splash!

rock and water design in gardens

splash!

rock and water design in gardens

peter robinson

photography by peter anderson

southwater

This edition is published by Southwater

Southwater is an imprint of
Anness Publishing Ltd
Hermes House, 88–89 Blackfriars Road
London SE1 8HA
tel. 020 7401 2077; fax 020 7633 9499
www.southwaterbooks.com; info@anness.com

This edition distributed in the UK by
The Manning Partnership Ltd
6 The Old Dairy, Melcombe Road
Bath BA2 3LR
tel. 01225 478 444; fax 01225 478 440
sales@manning-partnership.co.uk

This edition distributed in the USA and Canada by
National Book Network
4720 Boston Way, Lanham, MD 20706
tel. 301 459 3366; fax 301 459 1705
www.nbnbooks.com

This edition distributed in Australia by
Pan Macmillan Australia
Level 18, St Martins Tower, 31 Market St
Sydney, NSW 2000
tel. 1300 135 113; fax 1300 135 103
customer.service@macmillan.com.au

This edition distributed in New Zealand by
The Five Mile Press (NZ) Ltd
PO Box 33–1071 Takapuna
Unit 11/101–111 Diana Drive, Glenfield
Auckland 10
tel. (09) 444 4144; fax (09) 444 4518
fivemilenz@clear.net.nz

A CIP catalogue record for this book is available
from the British Library.

Publisher: Joanna Lorenz
Managing Editor: Judith Simons
Executive Editor: Caroline Davison
Designer: Kathryn Gammon
Editorial Reader: Penelope Goodare
Production Controller: Nick Thompson

Previously published as part of a larger volume,
Rock and Water Gardening.

1 2 3 4 5 6 7 8 9 10

Note: It is important to ask a qualified electrician to
install any outside power supply. The publishers
cannot be held responsible for any accident or injury
that may occur as a result of using this book.

CONTENTS

INTRODUCTION

Dig a hole in your garden and you begin a process that can change your life forever. Make the hole watertight, add water and you have a pool. Shape the excavated soil and use your imagination to add rocks, and a rocky water feature evolves. Add some plants, and a water garden is born. As soon as you decide to break away from the stereotype of a pool circumscribed by irregular paving or evenly shaped paving slabs, there are unparalleled opportunities to be creative with natural materials.

THE APPEAL OF ROCK AND WATER

Working with rock and water is an artistic process that does not lend itself to the quick-fix, self-assembly package. An artist knows how important it is to spend time on establishing the initial framework; artists do not take shortcuts or scrimp on costs at this stage. Simplicity is one of the keys to success in a good design, and boldness in the initial design is important. For this reason, explore all possible options in natural materials and be confident with your initial outline.

This may mean that a large part of your budget is used on equipment that allows you to use larger stones. Even apparently inaccessible sites can have large rocks slung in by a road crane, and a small cultivator can be lifted in at the same time to help with excavating and positioning. There are few schemes in which including a few large rocks will not have more impact than using a greater number of smaller rocks, all the same size and shape, and it is not true that larger pieces are appropriate only in large gardens: one large piece of rock in or near a pool in a small courtyard can have great impact.

No matter how small the size of the water feature, it is important to think about the selection of each rock, how it is presented to its neighbours, the way the faces are positioned, how deeply it is buried and which side is uppermost. If you do not take this trouble, the beauty of each individual rock may not be seen, and a substantial combination of pieces will quickly look unco-ordinated and unnatural. For this reason a gardener may be deterred from attempting a scheme that combines rock and water in favour of a water feature that can be placed in the hands of a landscape contractor or built on a do-it-yourself basis, where the skills required may seem less daunting. The rewards resulting from creating a successful water and rock garden are so great, however, that they more than outweigh any problems that the process may present.

The main essentials to creating a rock and water feature are having an appreciation of the natural landscape and, at a practical level, having some help in lifting the rocks if they are large. Every natural rock pool, stream, river or pool has its own beauty, and each person will interpret these features in a different way. Ideally, the scheme should carry the imprint of your own character, so there is much to be said for playing a direct part in its design. Once the rocks are in position and the water feature is established, it takes a brave person to dismantle the scheme to make adjustments.

It is essential, therefore, that the initial placing is right and that you do not rely on planting to disguise weaknesses. If you are happy with the skeleton of the scheme before any plants are used, you will be doubly satisfied when the plants begin to become established and clothe the rocks.

Working out the design can be one of

the most exciting stages in the process

of creating a water feature. It can be

PLANNING
THE DESIGN

very helpful to visit other gardens and

to look through books and magazines

if you need inspiration for a design

that will be suitable for your garden,

as well as for ideas on where to site

your rock and water feature.

OPPOSITE: **Once you have
planned the design of a feature on
paper, an understanding of how
rocks are arranged in nature can
be a great asset.**

INITIAL CHOICES

A rock and water garden does not automatically mean that there will be a small rock garden next to a kidney-shaped pool with a small watercourse running through the rocks. On the contrary, the use of rock with water offers a wide choice of schemes and tends to preclude only those strictly formal designs that are more suitable for gardens with straight lines and symmetrical balance. Including rock with water is generally easier in an informal garden, where there is a sense of freedom in the shapes that are used and where there are slopes, shrubberies, curving borders and plants in groups rather than in rows.

RIGHT: **The dominant use and placing of walling stones has created an individual water feature, which makes a powerful statement in what is otherwise an informal garden setting.**

BELOW: **Ambitious stepped cascades require cleaning and the removal of leaves to achieve an even film of falling water.**

STILL OR MOVING WATER?

The first decision to take, no matter what the size of the garden, will be whether to have still or moving water. Moving water brings life and sound to a garden, and can be either exhilarating or restful. Small, silent electric pumps, which are easy to install and cheap to run, have made it possible for fountains, reservoir features and watercourses to be introduced into the smallest of gardens to create a variety of moods.

The two basic methods of creating moving water are by installing fountains or building watercourses. Watercourses can be formal or informal, while slow-moving streams can be built without the presence of any natural slope. If there is a significant natural slope in your garden it will be difficult to resist the temptation to design a scheme that exploits the noise and glistening movement of waterfalls. In informal settings, the illusion of a natural stream running through the garden can be created and enhanced by streamside marginals and moisture-loving plants.

A flexible liner is so versatile that it is the best choice for creating an imaginative stream or cascade. Few gardens are so level that a stream cannot be incorporated in the scheme; all it requires are space for a base pool or reservoir and an existing garden style into which the stream can be incorporated. Cascades and rocky watercourses need a slope if they are to look natural, and the more room that is available for the water to change direction rather than fall in a straight line, the more successful the finished effect will be.

The expense of materials likely to be invested in a feature with moving water will be more fully rewarded if it can be sited so that it is visible from a much-frequented window. The play of reflected light on waterfalls adds much to the attraction of a watercourse. Keep returning to the window at each stage of the marking-out process, visualizing the angle and direction that the waterfalls will take.

MISTAKES WITH MOVING WATER

If the watercourse is to be an extension of the main pool, the level of water in the pool will drop each time the pump is turned on to charge the watercourse before water returns to the base pool. If the pool is very small and an extensive watercourse is designed to be pumped from it, the pool could be pumped dry. Do not design a watercourse with a larger surface area than the main reservoir pool. If the pool is topped up when the pump is circulating, then there is a risk that there will be too much water in the system and the base pool will flood once the pump is turned off.

Moving water may be introduced later on, and the design of a feature with still water ought to take this future change into account in its initial shape, position and size. A tiny pool, for instance, may not contain a sufficient volume of water to cope with the circulation requirements of a fountain or watercourse. If you plan

to add such a feature at a later date, make sure that the pool has an adequate reservoir by increasing the depth, even if it is difficult to enlarge the surface area.

SUNKEN OR RAISED POOLS?

If a still pool is your choice, decide whether it is going to be sunken or raised or partly raised. A sloping site lends itself to a partly raised pool so that it is possible to achieve the necessary level surround, and such an arrangement works well when it is edged with a retaining wall of rock. If the pool is to be sited on a slope that climbs away from the house, cut into the bank rather than making a retaining wall on the lower side of the pool. If you do this, the pool will not be obscured by the mound-like retaining wall and will, instead, be level with the land on the house side of the garden. If, however, the slope falls away from the house, build a retaining wall to make a partially raised pool with the retaining wall on the lower side of the slope. If you do this, the pool will be more visible from the house than if the bank were cut into and the pool partially obscured on the house side.

A raised pool on a flat site tends to be much more appropriate in a formal garden, but small informal pools can be incorporated inside old railway sleepers (ties) with small rocks and alpine plants placed around the water. This is an appropriate solution in small backyards and gardens where excavation would be difficult and where the size of pool is more in keeping with a tiny garden.

A sunken pool will look more appropriate in a larger garden where there is space to surround the water with bog gardens, beds for moisture-loving plants and rock areas. If a sunken pool is edged with rocks, using the same type of rock for outcropping on adjacent areas or for making raised rock gardens will make the pool appear much more integrated within the overall garden.

FISH AND FLORA

If keeping ornamental fish is a priority, it is sensible to consider that filtration may be necessary as the fish grow larger and their numbers increase. Filters require pumps, and pumps require electricity, which will be an additional cost in terms of both the installation of the supply and the running costs, and this may be a factor in your initial plans.

If plants are a priority, allow ample room at the sides of a sunken pool to develop independent boggy areas and ground for moisture-loving plants; the diversity of the planting can be increased over time. The plants associated with a water garden can take up more space than the actual clear water, and beds constructed with flexible liners immediately adjacent to the pool will very quickly appear to be an integral part of the water garden.

OTHER CONSIDERATIONS

There are other factors that will affect your choice of site for the pool. For example, the siting of a feature that needs a pump may be influenced by the installation costs of armoured electric cable. The style of water feature will also have a bearing on its siting. You may want to hear the sound of running water through a window or from a patio. Or, you might like to attract wildlife to the pool, in which case it should be sited as far from the house as possible. You may have a handsome tree that is a prime candidate for reflection in the surface of a pool, while the availability of space around the water's edge for future planting may take precedence.

FIRST QUESTIONS

When you are planning a water feature, these are just some of the questions you will have to consider:

• Do you want moving water?
  - If so, do you want a fountain or watercourse (or both)?
  - Will the main reservoir pool be large enough to cope with the circulation requirements of your fountain or watercourse?
• Do you want still water?
  - Will the pool be sunken, raised or partly raised?
  - Do you want a formal or informal pool?
  - Will you have to make provision for marginal shelves?

• Do you want to keep ornamental fish?
  - If so, you may need to consider filtration, using a biological filter and/or ultra-violet clarifier
• Is growing plants a priority?
  - If so, you will need to allow ample room for independent boggy areas and ground for growing moisture-loving plants.
• Is cost an issue?
  - Remember that introducing a pump, whether for filtration, moving water in a stream or fountain, or lighting will be an extra cost in terms of both the installation and the running costs.

MAKING A PLAN

Once you have decided on the style of water feature, make a rough plan of how you see the garden. This need not be sophisticated, but it should be accurate enough for you to position the pool in relation to existing items such as trees, buildings, walls and slopes. One of the useful aspects of carrying out this exercise is that it will prompt you to start thinking about all sorts of considerations that might not at first have seemed especially important. When you are preparing your plan, make sure that you include all of the following features before you even begin to consider anything exciting like future planting. It might seem laborious, but it will definitely be worth it in the end.

Marking the features identified in the plan below will allow you to see the areas that should be avoided if at all possible – that is, those in shade, those with underground service supplies and those in windy areas – while identifying the desirable areas of the garden: that is, those in sun and those that can be appreciated from the windows of the house. Only when

you have identified all the existing characteristics of your garden will you be in a position to get down to the more creative side of planning.

UTILITIES

Identify and mark the position of all underground services, such as water pipes, gas pipes, electric cables, drains, sewer pipes and manhole covers. If the pool is going to be excavated it is, of course, important that these are avoided. Most of them are deeper than the average depth of an ornamental pool, but do not assume that this is the case in your garden and plan to avoid them if at all possible. If you have no idea where they are, contact the company involved. The utility will have the equipment to trace the route of its pipes if no plan exists.

TREES

The position of trees will affect the siting of a pool due to the shade they cast and their falling leaves. The leaves of some trees, such as yew (*Taxus*), release toxins if they

A TYPICAL DESIGN PLAN

This simple plan shows the underground services, main areas of shade and viewing points. It is invaluable as the first step in the design process.

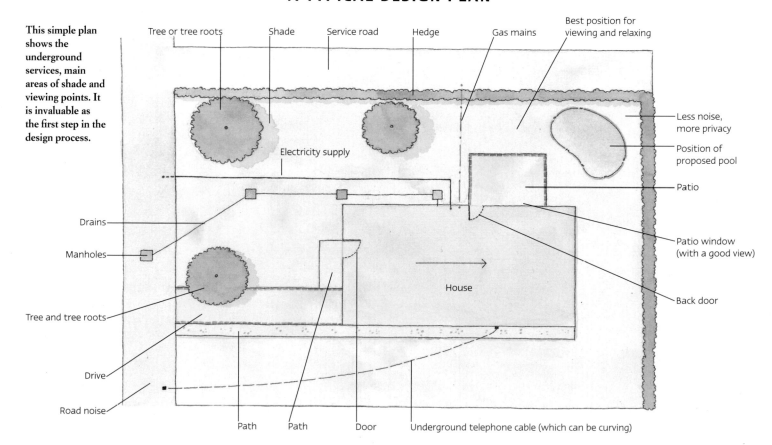

Tree or tree roots · Shade · Service road · Hedge · Gas mains · Best position for viewing and relaxing · Electricity supply · Less noise, more privacy · Position of proposed pool · Patio · Drains · Manholes · Patio window (with a good view) · Tree and tree roots · House · Back door · Drive · Road noise · Path · Path · Door · Underground telephone cable (which can be curving)

accumulate in water, so avoid areas near such trees. Also avoid siting a pool under most conifers because the leaf scales and old needles will drop into the pool almost all year round, particularly after heavy wind, and cause the water's surface to become dirty. The roots of trees can also be a physical obstacle to digging out the soil, and the questing roots of vigorous species, such as poplar (*Populus*) and willow (*Salix*), can damage flexible liners. Although some species of tree produce only light shade, trees such as horse chestnut (*Aesculus hippocastanum*) and sycamore (*Acer*) cast dense shade, and the area under them that is in shade constantly (rather than for a small part of the day) should be marked on the plan.

If there are any items with strong reflective qualities, such as a fine tree, mark them on the plan for consideration when working out the position of the pool.

BOUNDARIES, OUTBUILDINGS AND VIEWING POINTS

Walls and fences as well as outbuildings, such as sheds and garages, should be marked on the plan because they, too, cast shade. They also cause eddies of wind, which gust around the walls on an exposed site. The main ground-floor viewing windows are most important to include on your plan because they will help identify view lines. Doors inevitably mean paths to various points, and in a new garden it is important to establish the route of paths early in the planning.

WIND FUNNELS

Suburban gardens are notorious for having wind funnels between properties and fences. Even if you cannot entirely avoid a wind funnel, you can plant windbreaks or erect trellises in order to filter the wind. Filtered wind, such as occurs in the area behind a hedge or trellis, causes much less damage than eddying wind on the leeward side of a solid barrier. It is amazing that wind strength will be considerably reduced at ground level at a distance of from seven to ten times the height of the semi-permeable barrier on the leeward side of the windbreak. Aquatic plants make sappy growth, which is easily damaged or blown over, and waterlilies detest disturbance to their leaves.

ORIENTATION

It is important that you do not forget to mark the position of the sun in relation to your garden. Most pool plants prefer to be in full sun, and waterlilies will be shy in flowering without it.

ABOVE: **With due care in the design and in their siting, swimming pools can be as ornamental as garden pools, and can break away from the rather traditional rectangular shape.**

LEFT: **A large garden is by no means vital for designing and planting an interesting and attractive pond.**

THE WATER TABLE

There is one very important consideration that should be checked before you make any final decisions about your pool, and this is something that may not be obvious from simply looking at the garden. There may be a problem lurking underground in the form of a high water table.

The water table is the level at which underground water lies in the soil. It is likely to vary from summer to winter, being at its highest in the winter, even rising to within 38–45cm (15–18in) of the surface in some low-lying gardens. Its effect on a pool could mean that the excavation starts to fill with water to the height of the water table in the surrounding land, and, because a sunken pool may well be dug out to 90cm (3ft), this would be a serious problem. It is most likely to be a problem on heavy clay soils on low-lying flat land. It is less likely to be a consideration on light sandy soils or soils on the upper levels of sloping land. There have been some very surprised pool owners, who have woken up to find the liner billowing up to the surface

of the pool because of the water pressure in the surrounding soil. If this happens, placing heavy paving slabs on the liner or pouring concrete into the bottom of the pool is the only solution – short, that is, of rebuilding the whole pool in reinforced concrete.

FINDING THE WATER TABLE

If you are at all uncertain about the level of the water table in your garden, it is a sensible precaution to dig a trial hole on the proposed site. If the trial hole reveals a problem, draining the site is not an easy option and could be very costly. A soak away or drainage chamber constructed under or near the pool will simply fill with water, so consider other remedies before abandoning the idea of a water garden. If the garden has any slope, consider re-siting the pool on the higher land. If there is no slope, you might prefer to build a pool that is raised slightly above the water table either by elevating the pool sides or by building up the soil level on the

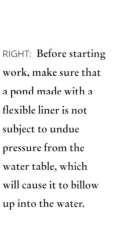

RIGHT: **Before starting work, make sure that a pond made with a flexible liner is not subject to undue pressure from the water table, which will cause it to billow up into the water.**

OPPOSITE ABOVE:

Natural pools, such as wildlife pools, are likely to look best if they are sited at a low point in the garden.

proposed site. Obviously, the latter solution would need to be done sensitively so that the pool does not look like the crater of a volcano. You will probably also have to import large quantities of soil to achieve a natural finish. Raising the walls of the pool is a more suitable solution in a formal garden or in a small garden where the surrounding contours are not so important.

EXPLOITING A HIGH WATER TABLE

You can exploit a high water table by making a natural pool with a gentle, sloping gradient around the sides. This can be done successfully if your garden is on solid clay, which can be compressed into a sunken saucer shape with a heavy hammer. The pummelling will make the clay less susceptible to the seasonal variance in the water table, and, as long as the water level is topped up in periods of prolonged dry weather, it will work reasonably well and cost nothing. Such a pool may be prone to flooding in wet winter weather, but it is possible to overcome this to some extent by a careful choice of planting in the surrounding soil. Such pools are not suitable for fish, however, which can become beached in the surrounding soil in a flood or parched in summer if you forget to top up the pool. As an environment for plants, however, it is second to none, and such a pool will attract a considerable variety of wildlife. Heavy rainfall may cause the water to become cloudy for a while, but this should clear in a few days.

LOW-LYING GROUND

The dream of creating a pool that looks just right in its surroundings inevitably leads gardeners to think about siting an informal or wildlife pool at the lowest point in the garden. If there is no problem with the water table, this is a good choice. There are, however, two minor points to bear in mind. The first is that the lowest point in the garden is invariably a frost pocket, and the cold air that settles there in winter and spring tends to delay the warming up of the water in late spring. Provided your planting does not include early-spring-flowering plants, which will be damaged by frost, such as skunk cabbage (*Lysichiton*), this need be no more than a minor snag. The second point, which is more serious in an area subject to flash rainstorms, is the risk of flooding the pool by water run-off from the surrounding higher ground. Although the flooding may be only temporary after exceptionally heavy rain, the floodwater may contain fertilizers or other garden chemicals. The addition of any chemical to a pool can have serious

HOW TO FIND THE WATER TABLE

It is better to work out the level of the water table in your garden in winter and after a period of heavy rain to assess the highest level that the table is likely to reach. To discover the level of the water table, follow these guidelines:

- Dig a hole about 30–40cm (12–16in) square and to the same depth as the proposed pool
- Leave the hole for a day or two to see if any water seeps in from the sides and, if so, at what level it finally settles

consequences for fish, and even a small amount of fertilizer can cause the water to turn green. Positioning the pool on a slightly elevated part of the garden will do much to minimize these two potential problems, and when the pool has to be drained, the water can be siphoned out to the land, without the need for a pump.

SIZE, DEPTH AND SHAPE

ABOVE: **Small, shallow pools can soon become choked with submerged oxygenators. The depth, rather than the surface area, has more bearing on a healthy balanced pond.**

OPPOSITE BELOW: **The shallowness of this circular pool means that it will need the movement of water, preferably through a filter, to prevent it from going cloudy.**

Restrictions already existing within your garden may give little freedom in determining the size of pool, but if there are few limitations on space, design a pool that is as large as possible. Apart from the greater impact of a large pool, it is an established fact that the larger the volume of water, the easier it is to achieve and maintain clear water. Often it is a lack of confidence that makes gardeners restrict themselves to a small kidney-shaped pool. Costs are, of course, relevant, but the cost of good flexible liners has become more reasonable in the last few years, and a glance at a price list of different-size liners will reveal that doubling the size of the pool does not mean doubling the cost of the liner.

DECIDING ON THE SIZE

Relating the size of pool to the size of garden is crucial. A pool that is too small will be insignificant; if it is too large, your neighbours will think you eccentric. There is no hard-and-fast scale determining the size of pool in relation to the size of garden, and any such scale would, in any case, become hopelessly confusing when it came to defining the boundaries of the water. A pool with sharp, crisp edges is a quite different water feature from a pool where there is planting both in the shallow water and in the boggy and moist ground around its edges. If the latter style is your preference, you will need as much space as possible, and you may find that the lawn becomes a mere grassy path around your water garden.

DECIDING ON THE DEPTH

While there are no definite rules about surface area, there are guidelines to the appropriate minimum depth, both for ease of water management and for the survival of fish in winter, and it can be helpful to understand the ratio between surface area and depth. If you visit an aquatic centre, you will see that preformed units all tend to be about 45cm (18in) deep. This should be regarded as the absolute minimum depth if you are making a pool with sides that are as near vertical as possible and if there are no marginal shelves. Take a closer look at the preformed units, and you will see that most of them have substantial areas of the sides moulded into shallow shelves. It doesn't take much of a mathematician to realize that the water contained in a pool with vertical sides and no marginal shelves will be much greater than the volume of water in a pool with slightly sloping sides and marginal shelves. When it comes to water management, the first pool is substantially easier.

Ease of water management can be defined as the ease with which a stable, self-sustaining ecological balance is created; in layman's terms this means creating clear water. Providing sufficient volume of water in relation to the surface area is the key, and the guideline is to provide a minimum of 378 litres of water to every square metre of water surface (10 gallons of water to every square foot). To achieve this in a pool with marginal shelves and slightly sloping sides, you will need a depth of 60cm (2ft). A depth less than this is an invitation to algae to spread; a depth greater than this is unnecessary in a garden pool of less than 28 square metres (92 square feet), and the water would be too deep for the effective flowering of most types of waterlily. In addition, ornamental fish do not need deeper water in temperate climates. Deeper pools will not cause significant problems, but there is no need to make work for yourself during construction. The main exception to this guideline is in the building of raised concrete pools for large specimens of koi, which is a specialized field of fish-keeping for which the guidelines for ornamental pools do not apply.

DECIDING ON THE SHAPE

The design of the surrounding garden will have a large influence on the shape of the pool. As we are dealing mainly with informal pools, strictly geometric shapes, such as squares, rectangles and circles, are the least appropriate. A kidney shape is the most common for an informal garden pool, and slight variations from this outline will help to give more individuality.

Whatever shape is chosen, bear in mind the practicality of later maintenance, and this means avoiding an excess of shallow inlets or promontories, which will soon succumb to algae and can quickly be completely swamped by the planting. If you have the freedom to make a wildlife pool any shape you want, consider an egg shape. It is strong and simple and has a wider zone, which may even be wide enough for a small island. If a stream or watercourse is envisaged, the shape will look even more natural if the watercourse enters a narrower zone, gradually widening to a more rounded outline.

In addition to the maintenance problems that arise if the outline is too squiggly, there will be considerable wastage if a flexible liner is used because it will have to be cut to fit the complex shapes. Liners can be welded into complex shapes by some suppliers and manufacturers, but this can add substantially to the cost.

The best way to decide on a shape is to lay out a length of string or rope or a garden hose on the proposed site. Some people use sand, but this is not as easy to re-lay if you change your mind. Not only is this process invaluable for deciding on the best site for the pond, but it will also allow you to refine the shape by assessing it from the main viewing points and at eye level, when it takes on a quite different perspective from that shown on the plan. When you are viewing the shape, bear in mind the future planting or any additional beds or rock features around the sides. Leave the string or garden hose in place for at least a day, so that you can observe where shadows fall across it. This exercise is one of the most important tasks in the planning of a new pool, and it is also the simplest to do.

The initial planning stage is almost complete. It is impossible to plot on a plan the placing of individual rocks, but a planting plan could be made at this stage.

Preparing a planting plan at this point may help to ensure that suitable areas are created in and around the pool margins, which may have been overlooked when the position of the marginal shelves was decided. In addition, if the plan is drawn to scale on graph paper you can also see how many plants the pool will accommodate. This is often frustrating, because it can soon become evident that there may not be room for everything, but many of the marginals can be grown in an independent boggy bed at the poolside and it is still not too late to make allowance for this in your final plan.

BELOW: **Decide on the shape of your pool by laying a length of string or rope or even a garden hose on the ground. Play around with the shape and design, viewing it from all angles, until you are satisfied with the result.**

AREAS AND VOLUMES

It is useful, even at the planning stage, to know how to calculate areas and volumes. These statistics will be important when choosing an appropriate size of pump and filter and in determining stocking rates of fish and oxygenating plants. It is also helpful if you need to use a chemical algicide to combat a build-up of algae.

Formal shapes present the least difficulty when it comes to calculating surface area and volume because they are easy to measure. Informal pools are more difficult because their outlines vary, and it is usually easier to base the dimensions on a rectangle or square drawn around the outline. Although the results are approximate, they are adequate for most purposes. When the water feature is such a complex shape that estimating the volume from one outline is not possible, divide the pool into sections, each with its own regularly shaped outline, and add these individual portions together.

CALCULATING SURFACE AREAS AND VOLUMES

Rectangles and squares The surface area can be easily calculated by multiplying the length by the width. The volume is obtained by multiplying the surface area by the depth. Where the depth varies – as in the case of a pool that has marginal shelves all the way around – divide the pool into two transverse sections, each with its own square area, and add the volumes of the two sections together. Remember to use either metric or imperial measurements throughout and do not mix the two. When you are multiplying imperial measurements it is easier if you convert inches into decimal fractions of a foot – 2ft 6in becomes 2.5ft, for example.

Circles Calculating the surface area of a circular pool requires the use of a mathematical constant called pi (π), which is 3.142. First, find the radius of the pool and square this; then multiply the result by pi (3.142). To determine the volume, multiply the surface area by the depth, making two calculations as before if the circle has two levels.

Irregular shapes For simple irregular shapes use the maximum width, length and depth to calculate surface area and volume as above. For more complex shapes divide the pool into approximate squares, rectangles, circles or semicircles and calculate the surface area of each. Add the figures together to calculate the total surface area. Multiply this figure by the depth in order to obtain the volume.

RIGHT: **You can easily work out the volume of a pool that is roughly circular by using a simple formula.**

LEFT: Large informal pool shapes need to be broken down into a series of smaller rectangles or circles in order to work out the volume.

CONVERTING THE VOLUME INTO LITRES OR GALLONS

The formulae for calculating volumes will give a final figure in cubic metres or cubic feet. To convert cubic metres into litres, multiply the figure by 1,000. To convert cubic feet into gallons multiply the figure by 6.25.

The first time you may need to use these measurements will be if you are going to use a flexible liner to make the pool. Remember that the all-important depth of the sides must be added to the length and breadth. A simple calculation of the surface area to give an indication of the cost of the liner would be a very serious underestimate.

If you live in an area where there are local suppliers who retail liners off the shelf, there is much to be said for digging out the hole first then going along to buy the liner. If you can do this, any alterations that you make to the original plan during the digging process, by either slightly enlarging or reducing the pool size, can be taken into account when you buy the flexible liner. If you have already ordered the liner from a mail-order source, you will have to stick rigidly to your original measurements.

HOW TO CALCULATE AREA AND VOLUME

Calculating the right surface area and volume of your pond is vitally important. The following formulae are for common pool shapes:

Calculating surface area
Rectangles and squares
area = length x width

Circles
area = r^2 x pi (r = the radius of pool)

Irregular shapes
area = maximum width x length
(Note: for complex irregular shapes, divide the pool into approximate squares, rectangles, circles or semi-circles and calculate the surface area of each)

Calculating volume of water
volume = surface area x depth
(Note: where the depth varies, such as in a pool with marginal shelves all the way round, divide the pool into two transverse sections, each with its own square area, and add together the volumes of the two sections)

Converting litres and gallons
To convert cubic metres into litres:
multiply the figure by 1,000
To convert cubic feet into gallons:
multiply the figure by 6.25

Remember to work consistently in either metric or imperial measurements

SAFETY

It is impossible to make a water garden utterly safe, and this may be a major consideration if the safety of small children is a particular concern. Short of fencing the water off completely and having access through a lockable gate, it is perhaps best to postpone building a dangerously deep pool. A design that allows for the introduction of water at a later date is sensible; you could even use the proposed pool area as a sandpit in the short term.

IMPROVING SAFETY

An existing pool can be made safer by making a safety grid that is strong enough to bear the weight of a child and that will sit just under the surface of the water. The grid, which can be made from wood and strong plastic mesh or from the galvanized steel mesh used by builders for reinforcing concrete bases, can be supported in the water by brick piers built from the bottom or on the marginal shelves intended to house aquatic containers of shallow-water plants. Because it is just under the surface of the water it will be quickly covered with algae, which will make it much less conspicuous, and plants can be allowed to grow through the mesh to disguise it further.

BELOW: **This purpose-built, plastic-coated metal grid makes an attractive safety net on a pond surface.**

CHILD-FRIENDLY FEATURES

There are also a number of simple fountain features that are reasonably safe because they do not have an expanse of open water. These include cobble fountains and small fountain spouts that emerge from drilled rocks. These are not only safer features where there are young children in the garden, but they are ideally suited to smaller gardens or where there is limited time for maintaining a more traditional pool. This type of fountain can be taken a stage further by introducing a play element into their design. A cobble fountain can be adapted to allow children to run through the water spout, or a variety of spray patterns, controlled by a simple timing device, can be incorporated into the design. Whether moving or still, water will inevitably fascinate small children, but it must not be allowed to become a source of anxiety for a young family.

Taking care in the design of the edges and margins of a pool can do much to ease any anxiety parents may feel if children are playing near water. If there is a lawn area nearby, boisterous children will often run from the grass towards the water's edge. The slope on this critical area should be gradual, both under and at the side of the water's edge. Many natural pools illustrate this arrangement: the surrounding land forms a shallow saucer, while the water level changes from very shallow to deeper water over a few feet. A man-made pool is much more likely to have a steep edge, unless safety considerations were high on the list of priorities when it was constructed, as this is an easy way of achieving a large volume without taking up too much space. However, a shallow slope towards the edge, as well as making the pool look much more natural and increasing the habitat for marginal plants and wildlife, presents far less danger to children to slip and fall suddenly into deep water. The risk can be reduced still further by creating a barrier of plants, including thick reeds and rushes, on the side of the pool where they are most likely to be playing.

This barrier planting does not need to be all aquatic planting in the shallows. Thick-growing, shrubby, suckering, woody growth soon becomes almost impassable if plants such as dogwood (*Cornus*), shrubby willow (*Salix*), hazel (*Corylus*) and elder (*Sambucus*) are chosen. If you really want a barrier while the children are young, use thorny subjects such as dog rose (*Rosa*

canina), holly (*Ilex*), gorse (*Ulex*) and barberry (*Berberis*). When they are planted thickly, species like these will look fairly natural near water. They can also be removed later when the children are old enough to be safe from any danger.

The choice of surfacing near the water's edge also needs careful consideration, particularly when there are elderly people and small children in the garden. Large, flat slabs of natural sandstone can be very dangerous when they are wet and algal growth forms a thin film on the surface. If paving is used, it is advisable to choose one of the concrete paving slabs that are readily available with non-slip surfaces; they are made in a wide range of sizes and colours. Cobbles, which will slow down children, are so unstable underfoot that they are not an ideal choice and are far more

likely to cause a fall near the water. If access is provided right up to the water's edge, make sure it is stable, and if there is any paving lay it on a mortar base to prevent movement.

ABOVE: **A dome made from plastic pipes and netting acts as heron protection. This could be adapted to increase safety for toddlers.**

LEFT: **A home-made, functional grid, just under the surface of the water and covered by cobbles, reduces the danger for small children until they are old enough for the grid to be removed.**

ELECTRICITY

The possibility of installing electrical accessories in a pool should be considered at the earliest possible stage, even if there are no immediate plans to include any such gadgets. It is so much easier to install cabling before the edges are laid and while there is still disruption from construction than to disturb a maturing water garden.

An electrical supply is normally associated with moving water where the source of circulation is an electric pump. There are, however, other electrical items that can be equally appropriate to a feature with still water, most notably lighting. In addition, an initially small selection of ornamental fish will soon grow and multiply, and a filtration system may have to be installed if you do not intend to reduce the numbers of fish.

There are few pools to which, sooner or later, an electrical connection will not be invaluable, and there are a number of precautions that must be taken to make this potentially lethal partnership safe. Before discussing the safety fittings used in an installation, it would be prudent to employ an electrician not only to fit the pieces together but also to advise you on which items of equipment to buy.

ELECTRICAL EQUIPMENT

The first item of electrical equipment with which you should be familiar is a residual current device (RCD), also known as a contact circuit breaker. Such a device should be considered as a compulsory installation rather than an optional extra to ensure peace of mind. These devices cut off the mains supply within 30

RIGHT: **By introducing electricity to a pool, an exciting new dimension of creative water gardening is made possible with the installation of a dramatic, cascading watercourse.**

milliseconds of the supply being accidentally earthed, quick enough to prevent a fatal electric shock. They can be purchased for indoor or outdoor installation. An indoor switch to pool equipment may seem an unnecessary luxury, but a cable can be taken through a house wall for relatively little extra expense, and the internal switch and RCD can then be controlled from indoors. For something like lighting, which is switched on and off frequently, an internal switch is a boon. For equipment such as filter pumps, which may be running continuously, there is less advantage in having an indoor switch because these would switch off automatically through the RCD if there was a problem.

From the source of the supply protected by an RCD the supply will need cabling to an outdoor connector or switch. Because the route of this cable is likely to cross part of the garden, there is always the risk that it may be cut or damaged when you are cultivating the borders. To prevent this from happening, use special cabling with a thick protective sheathing or armoured coating, and bury it deep enough to ensure that it is unlikely to be exposed during normal gardening activities. As an extra precaution, cover the cable with roofing tiles and lay a marker tape over these to alert any future gardener to the presence of an underground electrical cable.

The buried armoured cable is brought back to the surface at an appropriate point near the pool and connected to an approved waterproof connector or switch. At this connection box or switch the integral cable supplied with the pump or other device is also connected and the circuit is completed.

LOW-VOLTAGE UNITS

An increasing number of electrical accessories, such as pool lighting, are now supplied only as low-voltage units. The current to these accessories is reduced by a transformer to a level of voltage that will not be lethal in the event of a shock. The transformer replaces the RCD used with a mains voltage unit and can be supplied as a waterproofed outdoor fitting or, more commonly, for connecting in a dry airy place inside. Just as the RCD protection is not required, the supply cable to the accessory no longer needs the armoured sheathing, and cheaper low-voltage cable is all that is necessary. It is still prudent to protect this low-voltage cable in a plastic conduit. For some reason it is extremely palatable to mice, which can chew through unprotected cable in no time at all.

ABOVE: **Using three geyser jets, rather than one central jet, helps to blend the mix of formal and informal styles in this arrangement.**

ABOVE LEFT: **Even a shady spot can be brought to life by the movement of a waterfall and an abundance of shade-loving plants.**

LEFT: **This lush mix of leaves and flowers is given added emphasis by the spray of the fountain glistening in the sunshine.**

The finishing touches to a successful rock and water garden can make all the difference to its overall impact.

SPECIAL FEATURES

Many of these features, including lighting and fountains, can be added at a later stage in the construction process. However, it is really best to consider larger features, such as islands and bridges, during the early stages of planning and design.

OPPOSITE: **Features such as bridges and large boulders along the length of a stream bring added interest.**

DECKING

Wooden decking is one of the best surfaces with which to edge water where there is also a need for an outdoor living area. Unlike most other edges, a substantial overhang can be created to give the illusion that the water runs beneath the decking. Because wood is a natural material, it works well in an informal garden in which straight edges would otherwise look out of place.

Ecologically, a wooden surface has two distinct advantages over a paved surface. First, it allows rainfall to permeate the ground beneath, so that the decking can be built around any existing trees or vegetation, and there is no need to make special provision for extra watering. New plants can be introduced into the decking design by planting them into the soil below and leaving a small aperture, just wide enough for the stem to appear through the surface of the decking. Second, because it is very close to the water, the gap beneath the decking is an excellent home for amphibians, such as toads and frogs. The temperature and humidity in such an area seems to suit them.

From a landscaping point of view, decking offers endless possibilities. New levels, split levels, steps, railings and pergolas are all easier to attach to a structure that is basically a suspended wooden surface.

From a practical point of view, the void underneath the decking can be used to hide equipment and pipes, including ultra-violet clarifiers, biological filters, surface pumps, electrical cables, switches, connectors and transformers. Many of these items can be difficult to hide in a water garden that is dependent on pumps and filtration systems.

The surface of the decking can be made with long wooden planks or individual decking tiles. Both the planks and tiles are available in a range of different woods, but make sure that the surface is ribbed to reduce slip. The decking tiles have the advantage that individual tiles can be lifted for access to any of the equipment stored beneath them. The decking surface is attached to a sturdy wooden framework, which can be constructed to allow greater overlap of the water than any other type of edge.

Although a wooden surface is more sympathetic to an informal, natural design, it can accumulate algae in wet, shady areas, so it should be cleaned regularly with a very stiff brush. Decking is really more suitable for a sun-bleached spot, where there will be less algal growth and where the view will encourage you to sit at the edge of the water.

RIGHT: **Decking has limitless applications around water, particularly if there is a change of height, where it can be used for bridges, steps and sitting areas.**

OPPOSITE BELOW: **Decking planks have been used here to form a raised edge, steps and pathway around a pool with an unusual situation.**

FAR LEFT: Decking tiles made with the planks in a diagonal format make an interesting alternative to straight lines of decking and allow for easy access under each tile.

LEFT: The extreme versatility of timber planks is shown here, allowing a restful, sloping curve to be constructed over the top of this lushly planted stream.

FOUNTAINS FOR POOLS

Formal layouts, in which symmetrical balance, clipped hedges and straight edges are prevalent, are the most appropriate settings for fountains, which are more suited to circular or rectangular pools. A regular spray pattern from the fountain jet also enhances this formality. Where hot colours have been used in nearby foliage or flowers, the fountain will have an even more cooling effect. As plants with surface leaves, such as waterlilies, will dislike the constant falling water and associated turbulence, fountain pools tend to be very limited in their planting, confining this to strong erect marginals around the perimeter.

A fountain makes an ideal focal point and if it can be seen from the main viewing area, the droplets of water in the fountain spray will seem to come alive in the sunlight. This effect is enhanced even more if the spray has a plain or dark background. A windy garden is a problem site for a tall fountain or a fountain that relies on a fine spray pattern. Do everything possible to create shelter around the fountain and ensure that the diameter of the base pool exceeds the height of the fountain spray. This will not only create better balance from an architectural point-of-view, but will also provide a sufficiently wide receptacle for drifting spray. On very windy sites the problem can be alleviated by the use of a geyser jet which forms a wide, heavy and frothy jet. This is produced by a special nozzle which introduces air at the sides. A stronger pump is usually required to drive geyser jets, which are quite expensive, but enormous fun.

There are a number of interesting patterns available from the wide range of nozzle designs, and some of the main types are shown here. It is worth visiting a good aquatic centre where these are displayed in pools so that you can assess their suitability for your own garden.

Good maintenance is paramount with fountains, particularly those with fine jets which can become clogged very easily. Keep the water clear of algae and for a fountain pool devoid of plants it will probably be necessary to use algaecides regularly if there is a large surface area exposed to sunshine. In areas of very hard water, add pH adjusters to the water in order to reduce the build-up of lime on the jets, as the frequent topping up required in a fountain pool continually introduces more alkaline water.

OPPOSITE: **There is nothing quite like a fine-spray fountain for catching the light, particularly when it is viewed looking into the light source.**

RIGHT: **If a fountain is required in a waterlily pool, it should have a very fine spray to minimize the disturbance on the surface of the water.**

FAR RIGHT: **Create the simplest of fountains by removing the rose from a fountain head to produce a wide, vertical spout.**

FOUNTAIN SPRAY PATTERNS

Fountains are available in a number of different styles and shapes. The choice of fountain shape depends ultimately on the style of the garden. For example, certain shapes, such as a plume spray, are more suitable for a formal setting.

Plume spray: good for a formal setting

Bell jet: not very good in windy locations

Multi-tier: ideal for underlighting

Single spout: ideal for lighting

Surface rose jet: the simplest spray, often supplied with the pump

Geyser jet: good for windy sites

BRIDGES

When creating routes through a space, two different activities are taking place. One is directional, leading you towards an object or area; the other is spatial, separating one area from another. When these areas are separated by a change of level or by a barrier, such as water, a bridge can provide the route between them.

An attractive bridge not only provides a crossing place but also acts as a strong focal point, and is the true finishing touch to many an informal water composition. A bridge must appear to serve a purpose, and the simpler the design, the more attractive and natural it will appear. Bridges in Oriental water gardens have a much more symbolic function in the garden, and they are often brightly coloured or ornately built. The strong design of an arched bridge that forms a perfect circle with its reflection in the water is not appropriate to the simplicity of the natural landscape

that has become such a feature in western gardens. Regrettably, these arched bridges are often copied in domestic gardens where their steep arches tend to become awkward humps in a path rather than provide a strong reflection. If there is no need for the bridge to be arched, it will be much simpler to construct a straight bridge just above the surface of the water. This will provide a wonderful platform for looking down into the water and give a new viewpoint of the pool margins and their background.

Bridges can be made from a range of materials, including stone, timber, iron and steel. Building a bridge in stone is a skilled operation and should be left to a professional or, at least, a skilled amateur. Indeed, bridges across large expanses of water or big level changes call for specialist manufacture and installation. A simple timber bridge, on the other

BELOW: **Gentle curves and relaxed lines abound in this restful scene. The bridge is curved rather than steeply arched.**

hand, is a much easier affair and can be constructed with minimal building skills. Timber is a versatile construction medium. It is strong and can be cut into shapes to produce designs to suit a wide range of styles. It can be painted to complement or stand out from its surroundings, or it can be left natural, made in heavy sections of hardwood, and allowed to weather. The maximum span for an unsupported timber bridge is 2.4m (8ft); if it is longer than this it will be necessary to build piers in the water.

To bridge a small stream or bog garden, bolt wide timber planks to cross struts fixed firmly into the ground on either side with posts. Safety is always important, so sling stout ropes between these to make handrails, and attach wire netting to the surface to reduce the risk of slipping. At its most basic, rustic sawn timbers would provide a woodland look, but more exotic hardwoods would make this idea perfect for a Japanese-style situation.

Alternative construction materials are iron and steel, which have great strength, enabling large spans to be created. This is often used to support timber in larger bridges. The versatility of metal makes it suitable for both traditional and new designs. Sleek modern forms capitalize on the qualities of steel and wire, which combine visual lightness with great strength.

ABOVE: **Simplicity of design is perfected in this combination of bridge and plants.**

ABOVE LEFT: **A bridge made from larch poles works well in this country garden.**

TOP LEFT: **A bog garden has much more impact viewed from above.**

ISLANDS

RIGHT: **Islands can be a useful refuge for wildlife and can also be made into very attractive structures.**

BELOW: **This modern island design uses a submerged stone surround in order to create a line of reflection from the irises which appear just above the surface of the water.**

An island will add interest to a large, informal pool, and although it is better to incorporate such a feature into the construction from the start, a small island can be added later.

If the position of the island is included in the initial design, the outline of the island can be identified during the excavation. To create a wet island, leave a flat, raised mound just under the surface of the water in the chosen position. When the liner is initially laid over the pool, it should be drawn over the mound, providing a shallow area on which the island can be built. The island should be covered with a thin layer of wet soil, which will be a suitable place for marginal plants or grass. It will also be an ideal safe haven for waterfowl. To prevent the soil from

falling over the sides of the island, rocks should be mortared onto the liner around the edge.

You can also build a dry island for plants that prefer drier soil, such as trees and shrubs. To create a dry island, leave a flat, raised mound when you are digging out the pool. Drape the liner over the hump above the future level of the water, then cut the liner around the shape of the island. Any planting should be allowed to root into this dry soil.

If the island is an afterthought, however, drain the pool and build a retaining wall on the liner, following the outline of the island, until it is level with the water surface. The area inside the wall can then be filled with soil, which should be graded into a gentle mound above the water level.

STEPPING STONES

For narrow stretches of shallow water or streams, stepping stones make the perfect combination of rock and water. You will need to find flat-topped rocks or boulders. These will be heavy, so you will need to enlist some help to move them. Suitable rocks are available from stone merchants and suppliers. In fact, special large cobbles are sold for use as stepping stones or as isolated specimens on a cobble beach. Even if only one or two are used, stepping stones provide a highly pleasing way of continuing a visual link with the other side of a stream. This is best achieved when they marry up to other stepping stones laid into the grass at each side of the water.

Stepping stones are not suitable as a means of crossing water for the elderly, but they do make an excellent aesthetic and functional "prop" if you are creating the type of landscape that is associated with a natural rocky stream. If the water is moving, stepping stones can create ripples in the stream, which will add to the interest and exploit the fascinating properties of moving water.

If stepping stones are to be laid on top of a flexible liner, you will need to protect the liner with some spare scraps of liner or with pieces of black polythene (polyethylene). A wobbly stepping stone would spell disaster, so it is essential to stabilize each rock or boulder by placing it on a nest-like mound of stiff concrete.

Choose the narrowest stretch of water to place either a single stone or an arrangement of stones, because this will not only limit the number of stones that you will have to buy, but it will also look more natural, as boulders are usually held at narrow points, thus creating a dam.

If a stream has been built with one or more waterfalls, the top of a waterfall makes a good point to introduce a stepping stone because the width of the stream will have been narrowed in order to create the waterfall. As well as looking natural, this provides a useful crossing point and a good place to have something to kneel on if you ever need to make adjustments to the fall.

Timber rounds can be used as an alternative to stepping stones in a bog garden, where it will be easier to stabilize them than would be the case in water. It will still be necessary to bed the hardwood trunks on concrete to make sure that they are completely stable. If the timber rounds are thicker than 15cm (6in), then a hardcore base, rather than a concrete one, will be adequate. To minimize slipping on any growth of algae on the surface of the wood, staple chicken wire to the surface and brush over the surface with a stiff brush to remove any slime.

LEFT: The curving direction of these stepping stones, which meander through a dried river bed, is much more informal and restful than a straight line.

BELOW: This clever mix of flat-topped granite boulders and solid-looking timbers forms an enclosure for the waterlilies as well as an access path.

LIGHTING

Garden lighting adds a new dimension to any outdoor area, but especially when it is used to illuminate moving water at night. Consider the effect of a cobble fountain as its catches the light or an underwater lamp lighting up a waterfall from below. If you like architectural specimen plants, consider underlighting a giant rhubarb (*Gunnera manicata*) or an ornamental rhubarb (*Rheum palmatum*). The effect can be quite stunning.

If you have installed a pump in the pool, it is highly likely that a waterproof connector or switchbox will have been fitted already, so the cost of installation will be minimal. You will need to check if the type of lighting you envisage will be available in both mains and low voltage. There are an increasing number of safety directives limiting the use of mains-powered appliances for outdoor domestic use, and garden lighting is increasingly manufactured in low-voltage systems.

One of the joys of garden lighting is that it can be used to great effect in winter, when there are many silhouettes of trees and shrubs that are perfect for high-lighting. Supplementary lighting provides an opportunity to change completely the direction of the light source that illuminates the garden during the day, and you will find that features take on wholly new identities.

The surface of a pool that is clear of leaves in winter will take on a greater reflective role, and a good way of checking to see if there are suitable outlines that would be reflected by underlighting is to use a flashlight. Use one of the more powerful rechargeable flashlights with an attached plastic bracket so that it will stand up by itself. Place the flashlight under any trees, shrubs or ornaments that are behind the pool when seen from the main viewing window, and then return to the window, leaving the flashlight shining up into the feature. If you are pleased with the result from a strong flashlight, you will be delighted when there is a more permanent spotlight in the same place.

Of course, you cannot try this experiment with underwater features, but there are more obvious places for lighting: directly under a waterfall, for example, so that the light shines up through the rivulets of water, or near a water spout, such as a brimming urn or drilled rock fountain.

Avoid siting a light source so that it shines back into a main viewing area, and always hide the light so that the casings and lenses are not obtrusive in the daytime. If coloured lenses are used, keep these subtle: avoid turning the garden into a multi-coloured fairyland. Amber lenses are soft and will make a water spout resemble a flame, but they tend to bleach the colour from leaves so they are best restricted to non-plant features. When you are using a spotlight to highlight a feature, look out for lenses that will provide a narrow beam of light, which is useful for underlighting waterfalls, and for lenses with a wider beam, which are useful for bathing large trees like weeping willows.

An increasing number of solar-powered garden lights have become available in recent years. These are modestly priced and require no electrical connection. They can be used to mark the edge of an area of water or to highlight the route of a path alongside water, which is especially useful if the garden is used frequently for barbecues or entertaining.

OPPOSITE: **As darkness descends, the strong outline of the iris leaves will be clearly emphasized by the spotlight.**

BELOW: **A rocky cascade is illuminated by the lighting installed in this water garden, and seems to glow in the darkness.**

Water gardening has benefited from a growing investment in the materials suitable for a prolonged life under

MATERIALS AND EQUIPMENT

rigorous conditions. This means that the heavy manual labour involved in building a concrete lining for a pond or watercourse is now a thing of the past. In this chapter, we look at the materials and equipment commonly used for rock and water features.

OPPOSITE: **There is a range of rocks available for water and rock gardens, as well as machines to make construction easier.**

FLEXIBLE LINERS

With the style, size and site of your scheme worked out, now is the time to decide on the construction materials you will use. Concrete was once used almost exclusively for pool making, but then flexible and preformed liners were developed, and concrete is now no longer the usual choice for domestic pools, especially if they have an informal shape. Flexible liners are the ideal choice for the construction of informal water features. However, choosing a flexible liner has to be done with care. Your supplier will ask what type of liner you would like, and invariably the quality is linked to price.

Flexible liners are available in a variety of materials and thicknesses. Some materials were once manufactured in a choice of colours, but you can usually expect to find only black available now. The liners are sold from rolls of various widths, and, if installations are especially large or involve complicated shapes, they are welded. The most expensive liner is made from butyl and the cheapest from polythene (polyethylene), and in-between the two there is a range of excellent materials which are adequate for most applications.

POLYTHENE

Developed in the 1930s, polythene (polyethylene) was one of the first materials to be used as a flexible pool liner. It is cheap, available in different thicknesses and roll widths, and has a life expectancy of between three and five years. Its main drawback is that it deteriorates in ultra-violet light, which makes it harden and crack. For this reason, it is the least durable of all the flexible liners. Being a little unwieldy to handle, it can be easily torn and it is not easy to repair. Guarantees are seldom given with polythene, and you cannot weld or join one piece to another.

LOW-DENSITY POLYTHENE

In recent years, enormous advances in the manufacture of ordinary polythene (polyethylene) have led to a much-improved product, called low-density polythene, which is still cheaper than most other liners, but without the disadvantages of ordinary polythene. Guarantees are normally given with the two or three grades of manufacture that are available.

RIGHT: **The use of flexible liners allows for much greater freedom when you are working at different levels, as is the case with watercourses.**

TYPES OF FLEXIBLE LINER

Flexible liners are available in a variety of materials, thicknesses and colours, with varying guarantees according to quality.

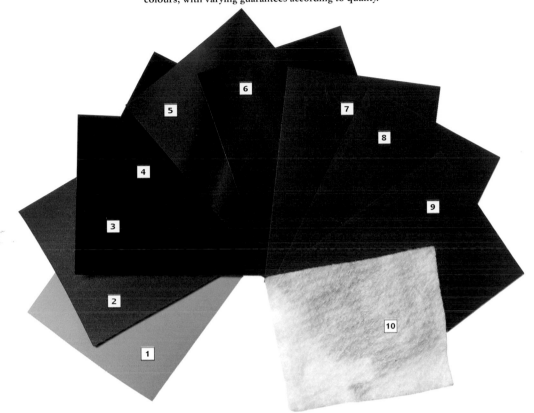

From left to right:

1 Butyl liner

2 Butyl liner

3 Low-density polythene (polyethylene)

4 Low-density polythene (polyethylene)

5–9 PVC in different grades

10 Underlay

PVC

About 30 years after the first polythene (polyethylene) liners appeared on the market, PVC liners became available, and these took off dramatically as reasonably priced liners that had overcome the initial difficulties that were experienced with ordinary high-density polythene. It has a minimum life expectancy of between five and 20 years and is available in different thicknesses. Some grades have been reinforced with a nylon mesh, welded between layers of PVC, for extra strength. It can be joined together, and easily repaired. The thicker grades are a little unwieldy to use in awkward shapes, but it is possible to get guarantees for several years.

BUTYL

At the same time as PVC appeared on the market, the real boon to water gardening made its debut in the form of butyl. It still remains the most widely used flexible liner by professional landscapers due to the fact that it has an elasticity that exceeds all other types. Because it is a by-product of rubber, it has the unique property of stretching under the pressure of water, and it will fit more snugly into awkward corners or crevices. It has an almost indefinite life expectancy, with guarantees available for 20 years or more. It is resistant to ultra-violet deterioration and can be repaired with a simple bicycle tyre repair kit. It is very simply extended by heat welding, and portable welding machines are available if welding has to be done on site. It is made in different thicknesses, but note that the thickest grade is very heavy, and you should make sure you have help in moving it about the garden. It is not the cheapest of liners, but it must be considered the best.

UNDERLAYS

Whatever type of liner you choose, it is best protected by an underlay of geotextile membrane, which is virtually impenetrable and, unlike newspaper and carpet, will not rot in wet soil. Soft sand is sometimes recommended as an underlay; this is perfectly acceptable on the pool bottom but is difficult to use on the sides and in any sharp corners, where it can be rubbed off easily. Like the liners, the underlay is available in several thicknesses.

PREFORMED UNITS

If you would like to have a small, formal pool with a symmetrical shape, a preformed pool unit is ideal. Such a pool is relatively easy to install and you will not have to deal with the bulky folds in tight corners which can be a problem with some of the thicker flexible liners. The stronger preformed units are useful for raised or partially raised pools because the walls are strong enough to support the internal water pressure and a more decorative outer wall can be built to disguise the unit.

BELOW: Preformed units can be used in conjunction with flexible liners to provide a base pool for a watercourse.

There are two main types of preformed units: rigid and semi-rigid. Rigid units are made of fibreglass or thick reinforced plastic; semi-rigid units are thinner and made from a cheaper plastic, which is moulded into sophisticated shapes under a vacuum process. Both types are better when they are moulded into simple shapes rather than being too fussy, with narrow outlines and several different levels. The regular shapes make it easier to pave around the edges and to disguise the plastic with a slight overhang of

the edge of the paving slabs. Fibreglass units are particularly easy to clean out and they need no more than a wipe over to remove a layer of algae if this becomes a problem.

Both types of preformed unit will have integral marginal shelves, which are positioned at the correct depth and width to support aquatic containers. When the containers are closely packed together and the plants become established, the rather artificial look quickly disappears.

Preformed units are less appropriate for informal pools. They tend to be built into fussy shapes with an excess of shelves, which reduces the volume and makes it more difficult to prevent the water from turning green. Most of the preformed units that are sold have a minimum depth of 45cm (18in), which is important for over-wintering fish and waterlilies during cold winters. A preformed unit that is shallower than this is best used as a small rock pool in a watercourse. This means that there is water moving through it, which will prevent greening as well as rapid fluctuations in temperature.

Although a beginner to water gardening may find a preformed unit tempting because it seems easier to install, such a pool is, in fact, more expensive than a pool of the same size made with the best of the flexible pool liners. In addition, although the units seem huge when they are seen displayed on their sides in a retail centre, they can be disappointingly small when they are dug into the ground.

SOME EXAMPLES OF PREFORMED UNITS

Preformed units are available in a range of different shapes and depths for both pools and for streams.

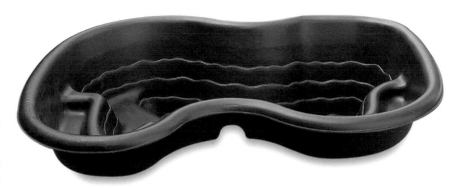

A unit with an even deep zone and ample shelves for marginal plants

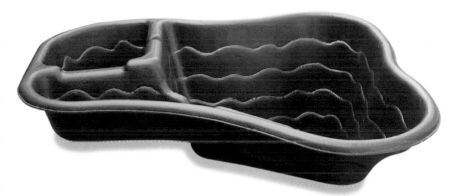

Less digging out is required with this unit which has a deep zone at only one end

A preformed stream unit cast from a gravel bed to give added authenticity to a pebble stream surround

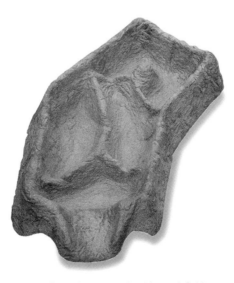

A preformed stream unit with a rock finish and a water basin with a right-hand curve

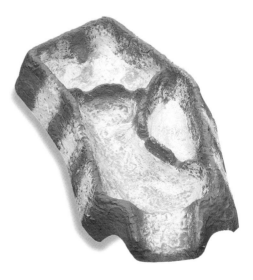

A preformed stream unit with a sandstone rock finish and a water basin with a left-hand curve

BUILDING BLOCKS AND MORTAR

BELOW: **Using bricks and a flexible liner makes for greater stability at pool edges.**

BELOW RIGHT: **Mortar can be used to cement rocks, here behind a flexible liner.**

BOTTOM RIGHT: **There are two grades of reinforcing fibres for adding to concrete or mortar mixes: fine grade (6mm/¼in) for skimming (left), and coarse grade (12mm/½in) for thicker layers.**

Traditional building materials still have an important place in building formal pools or deep rectangular pools for large fish, particularly if the pools are raised. The main change that has occurred in the use of concrete is that instead of moulds being cast inside wooden shuttering (formwork), concrete walling blocks are now used to form the sides and these are then lined with a flexible liner. Alternatively, the walls can be skimmed with mortar, and, when fish pools are constructed, the mortar may be given a final coat of resin.

Concrete is most likely to be used in the domestic rock and water garden in forming the walls of a base pool that has to be vertical to provide room for a greater volume of water and steeper sides for large fish like koi. The walling blocks would prevent the sides of the hole crumbling on a light or sandy soil. A flexible liner would then be used to make the pool watertight and disguise the concrete sides. On heavy, more solid soils and where the sides could be dug out at a slightly sloping angle, the walling blocks can be dispensed with and the liner simply laid over a sheet of underlay.

Materials based on cement have been used in pool construction since Roman times. They provide a strong, durable, rigid lining that hardens with time due to the constant reaction with water. Concrete pools are ideal for areas prone to vandalism or where flexible liners may wear excessively. Their main weakness is a tendency to leak through hair-line cracks caused by the slightest movement in the surrounding soil. The larger or deeper the pool, the more stresses are placed on the flat surfaces both from underneath and from the sides, particularly in soils like clay that are prone to swelling and contraction.

The use of fibre-reinforced cement, which produces high-performance mortars, has largely overcome these problems and eliminated the construction of thick layers of concrete in situ. The elastic, synthetic,

LEFT: **This excellent mix of hard landscaping materials in the foreground provides a hard-wearing surface from which to view the informal background.**

BELOW: **A small raised pool is an ideal candidate for using reinforced fibres in the mortar.**

reinforcing fibres enable a high proportion of cement to be used, giving a stronger mix but without the risk of cracking that would occur in traditional mixes with a high cement content. The thinner mortar layer allows more movement, and the concrete can be laid on sloping curves on the bottom of a pool without the slumping of wet concrete that occurs with a traditional un-reinforced mix. Despite the relative thinness of the layer of concrete waterproofing, it is very strong, absorbing stresses from the surrounding soil and eliminating the need for a foundation of hardcore or metal reinforcement inside the concrete.

In addition to using reinforced fibre cement to skim the inside of a pool made with building blocks, it is also extremely useful when rocks have to be secured to liners. When waterfalls are built, for example, it is often necessary to use mortar under and behind the rocks to prevent water from seeping behind the fall. In some water garden designs short stretches of stream may need channelling through narrow gullies, and this type of mix can be used to overlap the flexible or rigid liners and to provide a strong, watertight seal.

Mortar is used in several places in rock and water construction, but it does not take the skills of a bricklayer to point between courses of bricks and to watch levels. Fibre reinforcing is an aid to any unskilled gardeners attempting to build certain types of pool.

CLAY LINING

On areas of deep, heavy clay, a near "natural" pool capable of holding water for most of the year can be created by digging out a saucer-shaped pool to a minimum depth of 45cm (18in), thoroughly consolidating the exposed surface with a clay rammer, and adding a 15cm (6 in) layer of soil on top. If you do not have clay soil, then you can either import clay, which can be expensive, or use sodium bentonite clay and bentomat.

BELOW: **Clay lining is ideal for large informal pools, particularly if there is a constant supply of natural water.**

SUITABLE SITES

Clay lining is a relatively cheap and easy means of water retention, but it has a number of limitations in size, design and management. Such a clay pool can be constructed only in soil that is as near to clay as possible. Heavy, loamy soils, no matter how much they are consolidated, will not hold water in summer. Clay is generally identifiable by its "putty-like" consistency when wet, and its hard, almost rock-like consistency when dry. The surface becomes slippery when it is wet, but water tends to run off rather than penetrate deeply.

To achieve the compaction necessary to waterproof clay, it is not possible to have a pool with vertical side walls. Gently sloping sides must be contoured, and this means that the pool must be no less than 5–6m (16½–20ft) across in order to achieve the necessary surface-to-depth ratio. If simply left as a small, shallow

LEFT: A clay-lined
pool is sometimes
prone to temporary
clouding after periods
of heavy rain.

BELOW: This metal
tamping tool is
used to consolidate
a clay lining.

saucer, algae will inevitably accumulate in the warm water, and the drop in level in small pools in summer will be very noticeable. Not only does the clay absorb water, but water is also lost through both evaporation and transpiration from any aerial leaves. Bear in mind that the exposed clay will dry out extremely fast during excavation, and the surface must be covered at once with sacking or polythene (polyethylene).

The roots of plants such as waterlilies and some vigorous marginals will also penetrate the submerged clay and spread very rapidly. Extreme care is therefore needed in the choice of planting if the pool is not to become overgrown. Subterranean creatures like worms and moles may also burrow through the clay and damage the waterproofing.

Despite these drawbacks, puddled clay pools have their uses, particularly in rural areas where there is plenty of space and where they make ideal wildlife pools.

BENTONITE CLAY AND BENTOMAT

A recent development that refines the basic clay-lining method and improves its water-holding capacity is the use of an imported clay called bentonite. This is a mineral clay that absorbs water, swelling to 10 to 15 times its volume when wet, and that has strong bonding qualities. It has been used extensively by engineers to waterproof rivers and canals. The name is derived from Fort Benton, Montana, where it was discovered as a volcanic ash, and it is sold loose, under a variety of tradenames, in 50kg (110lb) bags.

When the bentonite is dispersed loose, difficulties can be experienced in achieving an even cover, but this problem has been overcome by impregnating a textile quilt with bentonite. The textile, known as bentomat, is draped over the pool mould in overlapping strips, 3.6m (12ft) wide. The mat, although very heavy, is much easier to use than the loose product and is rolled out over the excavation, rather like a flexible liner. When this layer is covered with soil and watered in, it becomes a sticky, impervious gel, which should be covered with a further layer of soil, 30cm (12in) thick. However, some calcareous soils affect the bentonite, reducing its ability to swell. It must also not be allowed to dry out once used because the calcium particles present in the mix of sodium and calcium, which shrink as they dry, are unable to swell again. If the bentonite is applied in powder form, rather than laid in textile form, the recommended rate of application is 10kg per square metre (22lb per square yard).

If fish are to be introduced to the pool, you will need an ample depth of pool and an adequate covering of soil to stop chemicals leaching from the bentonite.

PUMPS

ABOVE: **Electric submersible pumps bring tiny water features to life.**

If you are contemplating a moving water feature, such as a fountain or watercourse, you will need a pump. The great majority of pumps now sold are submersible models, which require no more than a connection point near the pool. With the exception of some more recently introduced solar-powered pumps, all pumps run on electricity, either on mains (utility) voltage or on reduced low voltage through a transformer. When you are buying a pump, make sure that it has enough cable to reach a suitable connection near the pool. Low-voltage pumps are restricted in their output and are suitable only for small fountains or waterfalls. They are supplied with a transformer, which should be housed under cover close to the mains power socket. Because the cable from the transformer to the pump connector does not pose a threat to life if it is accidentally severed, it can be hidden under the soil or paving. Mains voltage, on the other hand, must be protected in strong casing and buried to a depth of 60cm (2ft).

TYPES OF PUMP

Most submersible pumps come with a flow adjuster and a T-piece connector, which can be fitted easily to the pump's outlet. Once the size of the flexible delivery pipe from the outlet is known, an adapter can be selected to fit over the outlet socket to couple up with the bore of the delivery pipe. The T-piece connector allows the pump to circulate water in two directions, to a waterfall and to a fountain, at the same time. In this case, it is advisable to fit a flow adjuster to each pipe fitted to the T-piece in order to balance the different flow requirements. Delivery pipes are fitted to connectors by galvanized hose clips.

There are two basic types of submersible pump. A standard pump will operate a waterfall or fountain with a strainer on the intake to sieve solid debris. The other sort of pump can handle solids, and is necessary if there is also a biological filter in the pool. These filters need to run almost continually in summer, so the pump should be designed for continuous running.

Before choosing a pump, you should also consider whether its main purpose is to drive a fountain or a waterfall. If these features are ambitious projects, the pump for a waterfall will need to be capable of handling a great volume of water, while a pump for a fountain will need to create greater pressure than volume.

The other main type of pump is called a surface-running or external pump. This is situated above the water in a well-ventilated housing chamber. It is mainly used by fish-keepers because its running costs and capacity for handling large volumes of water makes it more suitable than a submersible pump in a fish tank. For the purposes of making watercourses through rocks, submersible pumps are adequate and easier to install.

Another innovation in pump design has emerged in the limited introduction of solar-powered pumps. As with any solar-powered device, the siting is important in terms of receiving adequate levels of sunlight, and at present these pumps are suitable only for running small fountains.

SITING A PUMP

The type of feature will determine the position of a pump. Although the natural place for a fountain is in the centre of a pool, this makes it difficult to reach the pump to make any adjustments or clean the strainer. In a small pool this may not be a problem, but in a larger pool the fountain can be supported remotely from the pump, which should be located at the pool side for easy adjustment.

Pumps should be sited at the base of a waterfall rather than at the opposite end of the pool because this increases the efficiency of the pump by reducing the friction loss in the delivery pipe. It also reduces strong currents, allowing the water to remain as still as possible, conditions which are appreciated by waterlilies.

In general, pumps should be sited just above the bottom of the pool on a shallow plinth in order to reduce the amount of sludge sucked into the strainer. If the pump is used in winter, raise it even higher so that it does not disturb the warmer water there.

Unlike a pump that is used solely for a waterfall, a filter pump needs to draw water from the maximum area and not allow localized pockets of undisturbed water to build up. The shape of the pool will influence this, and it usually means that in a long pool the pump is sited at the opposite end to the return pipe from the filter.

When locating a surface or external filter, above-water biological filters need to be placed at the highest point in the circulation system. They can be disguised by dwarf and prostrate conifers or hidden under raised decking. If disguising the filter is difficult, install a bottom filter, where a network of perforated pipes connected to the pump's inlet draws the water though the filter medium.

CHECKLIST FOR BUYING A PUMP

When you are selecting a pump, consult a specialist and be prepared to answer the following questions:

- What will the pump be used for?
- What will be the bore of the delivery pipe?
- If you are going to have a filter, check the wattage of the pump and find out if it is designed for continuous running. Some modern pump designs are far superior to those of older pumps, and minimize the running costs
- If you are planning a waterfall, what is the height of the header pool above the reservoir pool and what distance will the water need to travel?
- If you are planning a waterfall, what width of water will be required to form a curtain over the stones? (As an approximate guide, allow for an output of 227 litres/60 gallons an hour for every 2.5cm (1in) of width of the waterfall stone at a height of 1m/3ft above the bottom pool.)
- What is the capacity of the base pool? This is particularly important if you are introducing filtration or for waterfall pumps, which should not change the water too quickly. The flow rate per hour of the pump should not exceed the volume of water in the pool
- What style of fountain do you have in mind and what height do you want the spray to reach? A foaming geyser jet fountain, for example, will need a stronger pump so that the suction of air through the venturi valves in the geyser provides the frothy effect

TYPES OF SUBMERSIBLE PUMP

Modern submersible pumps have an enormous range of outputs. Check the running costs if the pump is to be used continuously. The pumps shown here represent a typical range.

Remove control unit and receiver

18,000 litres (4,755 gallons) per hour

5,000 litres (1,321 gallons) per hour

1,200 litres (317 gallons) per hour

FILTERS

BELOW: **Although well planted, small pools that are heavily stocked with fish will need filtration for optimum fish health.**

OPPOSITE: **The number of fish that can be kept in a pond depends on its size.**

As soon as a pump is introduced to a water garden there is an opportunity to incorporate a biological filter. These are not essential in a well-balanced pool, but if the pool is well stocked with fish there is a real advantage to having supplementary filtration.

BIOLOGICAL FILTERS

A biological filter is most commonly operated by a pump that delivers water from the pool through the biological filter, which is placed above water level at the poolside. Some filters can be fitted under the water, and these rely on the pump sucking the water through the filter medium rather than pushing it through an above-pool filter.

Biological filters work by converting the harmful nitrites that result from fish waste and rotting organic matter into useful nitrates as well as by cleaning the water of algae and debris. These large biological filters are housed in black tanks and can be extremely unsightly, so that hiding them should be a priority. They need to be large because they house a variety of materials that both filter mechanically and biologically.

In order to maximize the surface area inside the filter, where the beneficial bacteria will grow and purify the water, filter media are available in various shapes and configurations, including foam, baked clay granules, lava rock, cut pieces of plastic pipe and carbon-coated polypropylene ribbon. To achieve maximum filtration, water enters through a spray bar, which distributes the water over the layers and blocks of the different filter media, then it is returned, usually through a low-level pipe, to the pool. An overflow system is provided in case the system clogs up in heavily polluted water. Bacteria take several weeks to become effective and the filter must be kept on continuously.

ULTRA-VIOLET CLARIFIERS

These specialist filters, which are electrically powered, are extremely effective in controlling the single-celled green algae, and they operate in conjunction with a biological filter. They work by forcing the freely dispersed algae to congregate in bunches which means that the biological filter can collect them more easily later in the circulating system. Water passing through the filter is exposed to ultra-violet light from bulbs in the clarifier, causing the algae to clump together. They should be positioned so that the water passes through the clarifier before reaching the biological filter.

A BIOLOGICAL FILTER

A typical biological filter in which the water runs vertically through the chambers of biomedia.

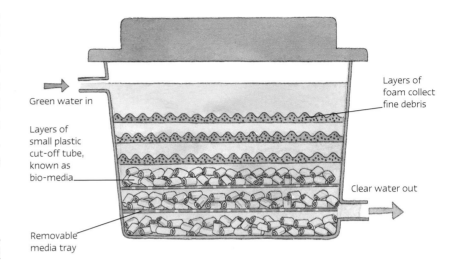

Green water in

Layers of small plastic cut-off tube, known as bio-media

Removable media tray

Layers of foam collect fine debris

Clear water out

A DIFFERENT TYPE OF BIOLOGICAL FILTER

This biological filter contains a mix of ingredients and vertical chambers, each with a different role in the filtration process.

AN ULTRA-VIOLET CLARIFIER

This detail of an ultra-violet clarifier shows the intake and output ports.

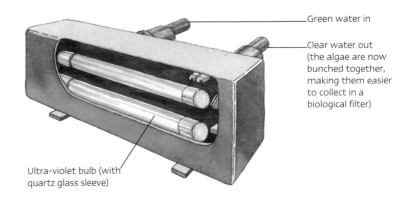

Green water in

Clear water out (the algae are now bunched together, making them easier to collect in a biological filter)

Ultra-violet bulb (with quartz glass sleeve)

PIPEWORK AND VALVES

There is a range of pipes and valves, mostly made from plastic, with which you will need to be familiar when building a rock and water feature. As time goes on, you will find it easier to use pipes, valves and garden hoses together.

PIPES

The delivery pipes for watercourses are usually flexible, unlike the rigid pipes that are used for small fountains. The flexible pipes come in a range of diameters, from about 10mm (½in) to 50mm (2in), and the bore required relates to the length of pipe and the role the water plays in the watercourse. As there is considerable friction loss in the pipe over a long distance, the rate of flow from the pump is reduced. It is therefore always sensible to err towards selecting a larger size if you are not sure, because there are no hard-and-fast rules when it comes to specifying which diameter should be used for a given length. Most pipes are now made in corrugated black plastic, which has largely superseded the clear plastic pipe that is also used for the purpose. The corrugations make the pipe strong yet flexible enough to curve around tight corners.

DELIVERY PIPES

Flexible corrugated delivery pipes are made from PVC, and are available in a number of different diameters.

30mm (1¼in) in diameter

25mm (1in) in diameter

20mm (¾in) in diameter

10mm (½in) in diameter

FOUNTAIN PIPES

Rigid fountain pipes of different diameters and lengths with a sleeve connection piece for additional length, if required.

10cm (4in) in diameter

20cm (8in) in diameter

ABOVE: **Fountains for pools require a rigid extension pipe.**

ABOVE RIGHT: **Watercourses need flexible piping to deliver water from the base pool to the top of the cascade.**

VALVES

You are only likely to come across two types of valves. The more common is a flow-adjusting valve, which is very useful on a watercourse. Although the pump may have such a valve fitted to the outlet, this is inconvenient to adjust when the pump is submerged. By fitting a separate valve in the pipe, you will have complete control.

The second valve, the non-return (shut-off) valve, is less commonly used and seldom necessary. It would be necessary on a suction pipe fitted to a surface-running (external) pump if the pump were not capable of priming itself after being turned off. A non-return valve might also be used in a watercourse where the end of the delivery pipe enters the header pool below the water level. Unless a non-return valve is fitted into the pipe, the water would siphon back from the header pool into the base pool every time the pump was turned off.

VALVES

Valves, such as the flow-adjusting valve shown below, are used to alter the rate of flow in a system.

Flow-adjusting valve or flow-adjuster
for altering the rate of flow

OTHER EQUIPMENT

Other pipes are used to connect delivery pipes of different diameters and to change the direction of flow in the system.

Galvanized hose or jubilee clip with hose
protector inside clip

Hose reduction junction pipe to connect
flexible pipes of different diameters

T-piece junction pipe to connect pipes
and change direction

BUYING ROCK

The edge around the water has the greatest impact on the overall effect of a water feature in the garden as a whole. Completely surround a pool with hard paving and the water is immediately separated from the planting and the pool becomes more artificial. In designing and building an informal pool that makes use of rock, you are immediately suggesting a more natural feature that requires sympathetic handling of all the finishing touches. Substituting pieces of rock for a paved edge is not the solution if the rocks are simply positioned on the liner above the water level, where they will look entirely unnatural. Position the rocks so that they appear to emerge from the water; they will look even more natural if the same rocks are used in the surrounding area.

BELOW: **The choice and arrangement of these large rocks and pebbles is in total harmony with the planting.**

The use of rock near to the pool is the key to success in blending rock and water. On a sloping site there is ample opportunity to use rocks in retaining banks and terraces, but even on a relatively flat site some types of rock will look perfectly natural if the rock used is the type that would naturally form a type of flatbed outcrop.

Before you finally decide how the rocks will be used, you must first choose the type of rock you would like to use, and then find out whether it is available and how much you will need.

RELIABLE SOURCES

Begin by visiting a good garden centre, where the rocks are likely to be displayed in large wooden boxes. The rocks will be of a fairly even size and weight so that customers can lift them out of the box to inspect them. If only two or three are needed, they can be put on a cart and transported home in the boot (trunk) of a car. Each of these rocks is likely to weigh 25–50kg (56lb–1cwt), so buying individual rocks will be a practical option only for small-scale schemes, where there are several smaller sizes mixed in the selection.

It is sometimes possible to construct a scheme by building it up little by little, adding outcrops at later stages, but if an ambitious scheme is envisaged from the very beginning, you need to organize bulk deliveries from the garden centre. As a rough guide, if you are building a small rock garden allow 2 tonnes (2 tons) for every 4.5 square metres (15 square feet) of rock area. This is not a hard-and-fast rule, because no two rock gardens are the same, and flatbed outcrop rock areas require fewer rocks than a terraced rock area on a slope. Remember, too, that a garden centre is likely to carry only a limited range of rocks in fairly small sizes. If the selection available does not satisfy your needs, your next point of call will be a landscape supplier, which you may also see advertised in your local directory under stone merchants or suppliers.

The selection here will not only be more extensive but it is also likely that when you visit the supplier, you will see the rocks displayed in bays in loose heaps. There will also be a wide variety of sizes available. Prices here will be quoted by the tonne (ton), and the supplier will deliver direct to your home. This source is infinitely superior to the garden centre because there

LEFT: **Where wide spillstones are needed in a watercourse, take ample time to select a thin piece of rock at the suppliers to ensure success at this critical point in the construction.**

is so much more variety in size, and it is this that will ultimately produce a more natural-looking rock feature. If you are building the rock feature by hand, you must stipulate a maximum weight. If you have some mechanical help, check with the hire contractor on the lifting capacity of the machine.

For ambitious features, for which a minimum of a full lorry load of rock is required, it is worth visiting a stone quarry. One of the joys of a stone quarry is being able to inspect old pieces that have been left lying about so that the cut surfaces will have weathered. There is also the chance that the pieces are lying on the ground for closer inspection (unlike the stone suppliers, where they are heaped into mounds), and it is worth talking to the quarry staff about the stones you find to explain why you like them and what type of stone you would like to form the majority of the load.

The haulage contractor is another key link in the chain, because careless tipping of the rock from the truck can result in several broken pieces. Try to be on hand when rocks are delivered, not only to explain where the rocks should be unloaded but also to explain to the driver how gently you want this precious cargo to be handled.

TYPES OF ROCK

For the best results, try to use rocks that are found in your local area so that the feature will blend in smoothly with its surroundings. There is a wide range of rocks to choose from, most of which can be bought mail-order.

SANDSTONE AND LIMESTONE

These are sedimentary rocks, formed in layers under the pressure of water above. They have numerous horizontal strata lines, which have weaknesses in them, causing them to split along the lines. These weaknesses can be exploited in rock-garden building, particularly if the natural rock formation has numerous vertical fissures as well. The quarried rocks produced from these formations, known as "freestones", are ideal because they have strong, natural sides. When one rock is placed on top of another, linking these fissures both horizontally and vertically becomes an essential part of the art.

Sandstone One of the best and most widely available rocks is sandstone. Depending on its source, the colour can vary from a light yellowish-grey to a dark reddish-brown. Although a strong rock, it weathers quickly, and the strata patterns look more interesting with time. It is porous, which can be both an advantage or disadvantage when used with water. Its porosity could be an advantage in wet areas with mild winters, where moss and algae quickly form on the surface, making it look mature in a short time. When used with ferns and moisture-loving plants in a shady place, the rock surface almost disappears in a very short time, becoming carpeted with a thick mossy growth.

Some sandstones are so soft in structure that the porosity can lead to problems in severe winters when the wet rock freezes and ice particles form within the rock strata. This causes the rock to split and break up over time, so it is worth checking with local suppliers or landscapers on a source of harder sandstone.

If sandstone is to be used to form a watercourse, check that it has a harder consistency and has had time to weather. It would, for example, be disconcerting to create a waterfall with large pieces of freshly quarried stone. The stones under and at the sides of the waterfall might turn a dark brownish-green within a week or two, while the surrounding stones, positioned away from the water, might remain a much lighter colour for several years. Although the lighter stones will gradually darken and blend in, it will look very unnatural at first.

York stone is another form of sandstone. It is quarried in Yorkshire and has varying degrees of hardness. Some of the best natural paving materials are produced from York stone because it not only resists wear, but is easily cut into thin layers, making it ideal for paving slabs.

There are several reddish sandstones, such as Monmouth and Cheshire reds, that are harder than many sandstones. Millstone grit is a good choice for a harder sandstone that shows the strata well. In the United States, two popular sandstones are flagstone and bluestone.

Welsh granite chippings

Sandstone chippings

Blue slate

Scottish quartz chippings

Limestone This became popular in the early days of rock gardening when the weatherworn, irregular shapes so common on the rocky limestone pavements of northwest Britain supplied the domestic market. Overquarrying spoilt this natural resource, and this type of stone can no longer be removed. There are, however, many old rock gardens, and these still supply the enthusiast who is looking for a special shape. Flatter, less weathered pieces are still quarried in bulk in Britain, mainly from Derbyshire, Wales, the Mendips, the Scottish Lowlands and central Ireland. The harder limestones suitable for rock garden building are carboniferous limestones, and they are mainly grey in colour. The exceptions to the grey colour are Mendip limestone, which is bluish or golden, and the Cotswold and Purbeck rocks, which are creamy, sometimes almost yellow.

The grey limestones are not quite as porous as sandstone, but they can leach a minimal amount of lime, making them unsuitable for placing near acid-loving plants. If they are in contact with the water in small pools in a hard-water area, the small amount of leached limestone will exacerbate the alkalinity of the water.

Marble, another form of limestone, is created when limestone is exposed to very high temperatures. It is too expensive to be used in rock gardens other than for cobbles and pebbles on a small scale.

GRANITE

This superb rock is very hard, fine-grained and non-porous. If it has surfaced in the form of glacial boulders, which have become rounded and smooth, it is ideal for placing alongside streams or in boggy meadows. Granite rocks lack the crevices that the alpine enthusiast seeks, but for a watercourse the rounded boulders are worth seeking out. Scottish quarzite, along with mica and feldspar, is an ingredient of many of the granite deposits found in Scotland. When crushed, it releases chippings which make valuable hard-wearing top-dressings.

SLATE

This very hard, angular stone comes in shades of grey, green and purple, often marbled with sinewy whitish streaks. During its formation, shale was squeezed so hard that the flaky mineral mica recrystallized at right angles to the pressure. This means that the rock splits easily into thin sheets, and these can be exploited when placed with a slight tilt on a watercourse. Devon rustic stone, a colourful slate, is very hard-wearing and readily available in block-sized pieces that are easy to handle.

Welsh green granite

Snowdonian slate

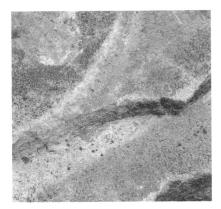

York stone

Devon rustic stone

Snowdonian plum slate

White marble cobbles

Red marble pebbles

Snowdonian blue slate chippings

ALTERNATIVE EDGINGS

As well as the vast selection of rocks and boulders that can be used to build a rock and water feature, there is also an array of alternatives you may wish to consider. You may, in fact, like to use a combination of different edgings, such as rocks, cobbles and grass edging, around the same pool or water feature.

COBBLES

If a rock edge to a pool is either inappropriate or too ambitious, rounded, river- or sea-washed cobbles can be used to make an informal edge. To look natural, they will need to emerge from a shallow gradient under the water, which means that they would not be appropriate for an edge with marginal shelves or steep sides. Cobbles blend well with other edging materials, so use them in association with these on just a part of the edge. Remember that a pool edged completely with a shallow, saucer-like gradient of cobbles will need to be much larger in surface area than a pool with steeper sides to achieve the same volume of water. There is also a greater risk of algae, such as blanketweed, forming in the warm, shallow water over the cobbles.

The popularity of cobble surfaces in modern landscaping has resulted in an increasing variety of types of cobble in various colours and sizes becoming available. It is worth visiting a good landscape supplier to see the selection available because achieving a natural "beach" effect is the main aim. Keep the general colour range the same and avoid introducing too many colours from cobbles sourced from different areas. It is not necessary to pay the premium for white cobbles, which are intended for more dramatic or formal landscape settings.

Washed, bagged cobbles can be expensive if they are used for a large area, and it is worth finding out about supplies from a local gravel quarry, which would be much cheaper. Quarried cobbles may need washing and will almost certainly have to be checked for split cobbles before they are spread on a flexible liner. Split cobbles have very sharp edges and could easily cut a liner. Large areas of beach could also be covered with a layer of 10–20mm (½–¾in) river-washed, rounded gravel, which is available in loose loads or bags, and this would be a suitable base for the larger mixed sizes of beach cobble.

RIGHT: **A grass edge looks natural, but will require more maintenance and some foundation support if it is subject to heavy wear.**

FAR RIGHT: **Irregular paving makes a good pool edge for both straight and curving outlines.**

In addition to the decorative nature of an area of cobbled edge, this zone will also act as a corridor for amphibians, enabling them to gain easy access to and departure from the water. You will also find that birds will be attracted very quickly to the shallow water to bathe and drink.

GRASS EDGES

An edge of grass can look the most natural of all edges, but there are several precautions to take if they are not to become muddy, unkempt banks. First, because an area of grass provides a stable place on which to stand at the very edge of the water, it is likely to become worn and compacted quite quickly. This compaction can lead to crumbling sides under the liner on light sandy soils, and any grass growing below the waterline becomes impossible to mow.

The other drawback that is associated with grass sides to pools is the problem of grass clippings flying into the water when the grass is cut. This becomes a management problem, which can be resolved only by the type of grasscutter used. There are a number of lawnmowers that are effective at gathering the cut grass in a box or a bag.

PAVING

Even in informal designs, there are occasions where a part of the pool edge will look quite natural when it is edged with paving, particularly if a path leads to the paved edge across a lawn or through a border. How well the paving is integrated into an informal design for water will depend on how much of the edge is paved, and the type of paving used. It is only when the entire edge is paved that the pool begins to lose its informality and its relationship with the immediate surrounds of the garden.

For informal shapes, the irregular style sometimes known as "crazy paving" tends to be the most suitable choice because the cut pieces of natural stone allow a curved edge to be created more easily than is possible with square or rectangular paving stones. There are also several colours available in the stones that are used for crazy paving, and some colours will blend better with the rock used elsewhere in the water garden. Many edges of crazy paving are spoiled by bad laying, particularly in the pointing of the mortar where it is used too liberally. A good area of crazy paving will have a balanced mix of sizes, the pieces will be laid flat and firm, and the pointing will not dominate.

ABOVE: **This pool edge uses timber rounds, which are sunk into a thin, shallow trench and then secured with concrete.**

LEFT: **This cobble "beach" edge uses cobbles of mixed sizes, which makes the finished effect look much more natural.**

There are several alternatives to irregular paving in both natural stone and simulated stone slabs. The main requirements for a paved edge are that it should be level, as non-slip and natural looking as possible, and the colour should blend rather than make a vivid contrast.

Building your rock and water feature is where the design and planning is put into practice. In this chapter, the

CONSTRUCTING ROCK AND WATER GARDENS

practical step-by-step sequences are accompanied by a list of the materials and equipment that you will need. The vast majority of the projects require little in the way of do-it-yourself skills, but specific building skills are identified where necessary.

OPPOSITE: **This unbroken curtain of water shows what can be achieved through the careful attention to surfaces and levels.**

INITIAL EXCAVATION

Firstly, you will not need a plug for drainage in the bottom of your proposed pool. The pool is not going to be drained regularly like a bath, and there is always a danger that the plug may not be 100 per cent water-tight. Plugs are necessary only in pools for keeping fish such as specimen koi, where regular cleaning out is necessary.

When you are digging out a new pool in a lawn or an area of rough turf there are three distinct layers to be removed, each one having a different function later. The top layer of turf should be removed to no deeper than about 5cm (2in), and, if space is available in the garden, the turves should be stacked in a neat pile. Arrange them upside down, and after a few months they will have rotted down to produce a superb fibrous loam, which is ideal for potting aquatic plants.

The next layer, the topsoil, is about 30–38cm (12–15in) deep and it, too, could be valuable depending on the soil type. If it is heavy clay it will have few uses; keep a small supply for helping to seal minor leaks in a replenishing system. Similarly, at the other end of the scale a sandy soil is of little value as future

RIGHT: **This new pool is made with a flexible liner and is at the stage of being filled with water. It is important to pay particular attention to levels so that the liner is not exposed above the water line. This is a good time to plant the oxygenators before it becomes so deep that waders are required.**

FAR LEFT: **When you are digging out a new pool in a lawn, you will need to remove a layer of turf first.**

LEFT: **When you are excavating a new pool or stream, remember to keep some of the excavated soil to build up the contours along the edges.**

compost or top-dressing. If the soil is a nice friable loam, however, it is worth its weight in gold and should be either used to top-dress the borders or stacked, like the turves, for future use. Finally, the bottom layer or subsoil, which is generally a different colour from the topsoil, should be kept only if you have plans to change any garden contours later on, when it should be stored separately from the topsoil. If you do not plan to use the subsoil, dispose of it; do not add it to your borders or beds elsewhere in the garden.

If a rock and water feature is envisaged, hang on to every barrowful of soil, topsoil and subsoil, until the scheme has been created. The subsoil can be placed at the bottom of a gently contoured mound and the topsoil returned on top of it. If this mound is made near the pool it could make a perfect start for a raised watercourse. The main thing is to stop the mound from looking too contrived, particularly on a flat site, by keeping the proportions and gradient as natural looking as possible. The height of the mound should be no more than one-fifth of its width, and it should have gently sloping sides. Small, steep, circular mounds covered with rocks positioned at various angles will look completely unnatural. They look even worse if the water spouts from the top of the mound rather like an erupting volcano.

SOIL PROFILE

A typical soil profile usually consists of three main elements: an upper layer of dark, fertile topsoil; a middle layer of lighter, infertile subsoil; and a lower layer of bedrock, which ranges from a few to hundreds of yards deep.

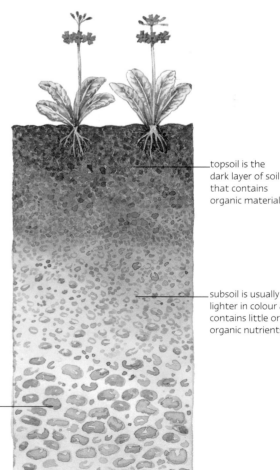

topsoil is the dark layer of soil that contains organic material

subsoil is usually lighter in colour and contains little or no organic nutrients

bedrock is usually below the level of cultivation

POSITIONING ROCKS

A good, natural-looking arrangement of rocks in the surrounding area is one of the most important aspects of construction, which can make or break the success of a pool or other rock and water feature. Without this attention to detail in the choice and position of materials in the surrounding area, a successful feature can be spoilt.

When you have chosen a design for the scheme and selected the type of rock to use, the actual positioning of the rock should be undertaken with as much care as any aspect of the excavation. The elements that will be in the background are as important as the pool itself, and it is easy to become preoccupied with the mechanics of the pool and fail to capitalize on the qualities that give water its appeal.

First of all, you will need to decide whether this is a job you can do yourself or whether you will require help. The size of the rocks will make the decision for you, but there is much to be said for having help, even if you feel that you can manhandle the rocks yourself. Placing rocks involves a great deal of moving to and fro, as you step back some distance from each one to view its effect from a distance. You cannot possibly assess whether the rock is sitting correctly when you are working on top of it. The slightest adjustment in the angle at which it is placed or the depth to which it is buried will have a profound effect on its success, and if there is someone to help make these fine adjustments, it will save a lot of walking about to check from various angles.

MOVING ROCKS

A sack trolley is invaluable for moving heavy rocks around the garden and into place.

1 Roll the rock onto the trolley platform so that the weight is pivoted over the wheels when it is being moved.

2 Pull the handles back in order to manoeuvre the heavy rock more easily.

CREATING ROCK FORMATIONS

You may need outside help to move larger pieces of rock into place, but if you are moving rock yourself, there are certain principles for positioning and grouping rocks that will ensure you achieve a natural-looking formation, largely by taking into account such factors as the shape of the rock as well as the strata that run through rock.

1 Where the slope is steeper, choose blocky rocks rather than flat ones.

2 In groups of three, a cluster of rocks with tops parallel to each other have greater impact and naturalness.

3 When positioning angular rocks, aim to keep the top of the rocks parallel to each other.

4 By burying a large part of the rock, an outcrop looks more natural than if it is sitting on the surface.

Once the first rock is in position, all the other rocks must relate to it so that it looks natural, and as the number of rocks increases, constant checking is ever more important. If the rocks look menacingly heavy, try every possible means to get a small excavator as well as a skilled driver on the site. Skilled drivers who know how to cradle the rocks in slings beforehand so that they can be lowered gently into place are worth their weight in gold.

POSITIONING ROCKS ON A FLAT SITE

A feature on a steep slope will need ample supplies of rock to make terracing, but avoid using too much rock on a flatter site. Remember that you are trying to achieve a setting for water, rather than a collection of rocks, and water works best if it is not overly dominated by the rock. Outcropping with clusters of rocks is a successful way of using rock on flat sites. Even though the positioning of adjacent rocks in a cluster will need careful placement, this care will result in a more successful scheme than single rocks of the same size scattered evenly around. Where single rocks are used, they should be big. Indeed, large, rounded boulders that appear to have been deposited centuries ago look superb, particularly alongside a stream.

POSITIONING ROCKS ON A SLOPING SITE

For more ambitious landscaping schemes that include a slope, flat-topped rocks that suggest the strata of natural rock formations work well. Having placed the first stone at the bottom of a slope, line up the faces of any adjoining rocks so that they are at the same level and face the stones in the same direction. As you build up the slope, keep the same distribution of rock faces and their tops, and it is for this reason that flat-topped rocks work much better. Angular pieces, with points sticking in the air and no suggestion of natural strata, can easily look a complete mess and spoil the water garden rather than providing an appropriate setting for it.

Imagine a wall of outcropping strata and attempt to simulate this. When you are positioning a rock, cut into the base of the slope so that the rock tilts slightly backwards into the slope. Pack soil around the back of the rock so that no more than two-thirds of the rock is exposed. If the slope is steep and the rock face needs to be terrace-like, the front faces of the rocks in the next layer should be set slightly back from the rocks beneath them, but still follow the all-important near-horizontal and vertical strata that were established by the very first stone at the bottom of the slope.

CONSTRUCTING EDGES

Choosing a successful co-ordination of the materials to make the edge of a pool is helped by visiting a supplier with a wide range of materials. The construction can then be approached with the confidence that not only will the colours and textures work well, but other rocks for waterfalls and streams would make a suitable combination. Whatever material is chosen, the rule in pool construction is to hide the gap of liner at the surface around the pool which becomes even more conspicuous in the summer with increased evaporation.

Rock edging The rocks around a pool should be partially submerged to achieve a natural effect. The rocks will also need to be supported on a foundation slab. The liner is passed over the slab and the rock bedded into a layer of stiff mortar or concrete. Ensure the liner finishes above the level of the water at the side of the pool.

ABOVE: **This is a well-chosen and carefully positioned mix of boulders and rocks; the boulders can also be used as a crossing point.**

Cobble edging The first essential in introducing naturalness to a cobble edge is to arrange the sizes so that the main body of cobbles increases in diameter from below the waterline into the drier margins. To prevent the cobbles from rolling to the pool bottom, a concrete support should be constructed at the edge of the pool.

Grass edging An edge of grass is very natural-looking and very suitable for a wildlife pool. However, the edge of the pool will become worn fairly quickly, which can cause the sides to crumble. This can be avoided by underpinning the turf with a small foundation.

Timber edging An alternative method of taking grass to the water's edge is to construct a vertical timber wall, which will extend from below the waterline to just below the level of the grass. The timber wall looks most attractive if it is made with timber rounds, 5–8cm (2–3in) in diameter, which are placed tightly side by side to form a palisade-like barrier. Proprietary lengths of "log roll" could also be used instead of complete rounds, and these are already joined together by galvanized wire strands. For both these systems to be made stable enough to prevent any crumbling into the pool, a small trench, about 15cm (6in) deep and 10–15cm (4–6in) wide, must be dug out at the pool edge. A concrete support should be added in front of this trench. The pool liner is then run over the concrete support and into the trench before finishing above the waterline beyond the trench. A mix of stiff mortar is placed on the liner and the timbers bedded into the stiff mortar before it hardens. Make sure that the timber rounds are straight and tight together because they cannot be moved once the mortar sets. After a day or two, when the mortar will have set hard, soil can be backfilled behind the timber edge and the liner can be wedged upright so it is held above the waterline. Turf can then be laid right up to the timber edge on the fresh soil, which is now supported at the water's edge.

Paved edging Prepare the area to be paved by scraping away some topsoil. If the subsoil is not firm, remove this too and replace it with 8–10cm (3–4in) of hardcore. Top this with about 5cm (2in) of damp sand, which must be raked and levelled, then cover with the

underlay and liner. Begin by placing the perimeter pieces along the edge of the water, checking that they fit well together and that they overlap the water by 2.5–5cm (1–2in). Use the largest of the pieces to give extra stability, with the straight edge overlapping the water. If you are laying on a curved edge, however, the shortest side might have to be used over the water to give a gentle angle for the curve. Mix some mortar on a nearby hard surface or board, then lay the first stones onto dabs of mortar trowelled onto the liner. Press the slab down onto the mortar dabs and bed it firmly before laying the adjacent slabs. Check the slabs are level with a spirit level. To adjust the height, tap with a club hammer over a block of wood. The gaps between the slabs must be filled with a fairly wet mortar mix to hold each slab in place. They should be laid on a slight slope to reduce run-off from any adjacent paving or grass.

ROCK EDGING

A rock used as a pool edge is best partially submerged with a foundation slab under the liner.

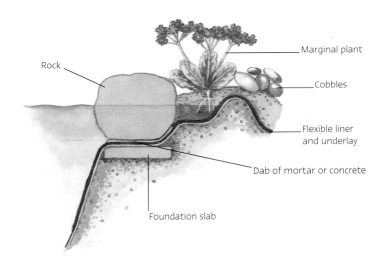

GRASS EDGING

A grass edge is subject to heavy wear and tear.
It should be supported by a natural stone walling block which is placed on a deep foundation of stiff mortar or concrete.

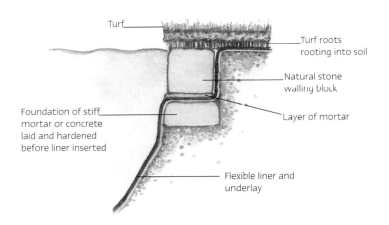

COBBLE EDGING

To prevent cobbles from rolling into the deeper zone of the pond, a shallow shelf should be made with the kerb under the flexible liner in order to give extra stability.

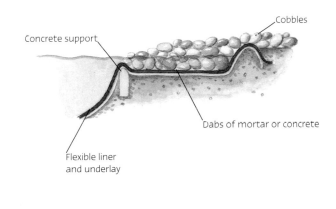

TIMBER EDGING

Log roll or individual timber rounds placed side by side make a good edge when mortared into a thin trench just under the level of the water. Turf edging can then run up to the timber edging.

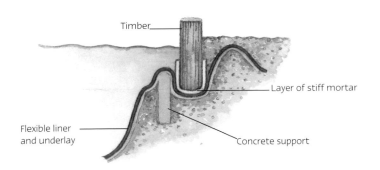

PAVED EDGING

When using a paving slab to provide an edge, ensure that there is a small overlap above the water, and mortar the slab onto the liner above a foundation of hardcore.

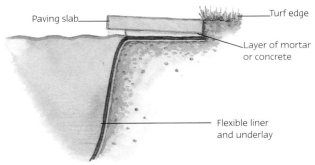

MAKING A POOL
with a flexible liner

YOU WILL NEED

- Garden hose, rope or sand
- Spade
- Polythene (polyethylene) sheet
- Rake
- Spirit level
- Straight-edged piece of wood
- Sand or underlay
- Flexible liner
- Bricks or heavy stones
- Large scissors
- Paving for pool surround
- Ready-mix mortar
- Mortaring trowel

The versatility of flexible liners has made them the most popular of materials for a variety of applications. They provide the greatest scope for pool design, and can be used on their own for informal pools on heavy soils or for formal pools where crisper definition and better stability around the edges are needed. They can also be used with concrete or walling blocks to secure the sides of an excavation. Liners are now so widely obtainable that you can dig out the pool and make a multitude of last-minute adjustments to the shape and depth before buying.

CALCULATING THE SIZE OF LINER
The most common mistake in calculating the size of liner is to forget to allow for the depth of the sides and for a slight overlap. Aquatic centres supply liners from rolls, and you may gain a slight increase in size free of charge when the liner is cut. Liners bought by mail order are usually the exact size, so it is vital that your measurements are correct.

To calculate the size of the liner, measure a rectangle that encloses the shape of the pool. After measuring the maximum length and breadth, measure the depth of the pool and add twice that measurement to each dimension.

The measurements for length and width represent the bare minimum of liner required. It is prudent to add about 30cm (12in) to each measurement to provide a small overlap of 15cm (6in) on each side. For brimming or reflective pools, where the surface of the water has to be level with the surrounding edge, it will be necessary to add a little more than the width of the paving or bricks that will edge the pool to provide enough liner to extend beneath and behind this edging. The end of the liner will finish by being held vertically behind the edging material.

One rectangle of liner can be used for a variety of pool shapes, including designs with narrow waists to make a crossing point

to add interest, for example. Where the wastage would be excessive for very narrow sections, smaller joining pieces of some types of liner can be welded together at specialist suppliers or taped together on site using proprietary waterproof joining tapes. Large creases in the corners of rectangular pools or sharp curves in informal shapes are inevitable, but they can be made to look less conspicuous if the liner is carefully folded before filling the pool. A covering of algae and submerged planting will eventually disguise the fold almost entirely.

If there is ample surplus liner, features such as bog gardens can be made around the sides. When a kidney-shaped pool is created, a small bog area can be achieved using the corner piece of a rectangular liner. Instead of cutting off the surplus liner, place soil on the liner and prevent it from spreading into the water of the main pool by a small submerged retaining wall of inverted turves, rocks or walling stones.

deep or a further 38cm (15in) if the pond is to be 60cm (24in) deep. The soil from this deeper zone will be subsoil and can also be used later if it is placed underneath any fresh topsoil. It should not become mixed with the freshly excavated topsoil. If you do not envisage using this subsoil later, then remove it from the site.

3 Rake the bottom of the pond to achieve a level surface. A spirit level on a straight-edged piece of wood supported by a vertical piece of wood will show levels. Smooth over the entire surface by raking the bottom to remove any sharp stones. Go over the sides with your hands, removing any protruding roots or sharp-edged objects, gently firming the surface by patting. Line the pool with about 1cm (½in) of damp sand – it should stick to the sides if they slope slightly. If the soil is stony, drape a piece of underlay across the hole and the shelves, leaving an overlap around the pool of about 30cm (12in). Lay the flexible liner over the sand or underlay.

4 Place temporary weights, such as bricks or heavy stones, on the edges of the liner so that it is not blown back into the pool. Before the water is poured in, check that there is ample liner above the edge of the pool all the way round. Fill the pool with water to within a few centimetres (inches) of the finished level so that any adjustments to the level of the sides can be made by adding or removing soil behind the liner.

5 The bricks or stones temporarily holding the edges of the liner can be removed. Build any edging before the water is filled to the final level. Never trim the surplus liner until you are completely sure that the water level and edging are satisfactory. This pool is to have a paved edge, so cut away the surplus liner and underlay, leaving an overlap around the edge of about 15cm (6in) to be covered by the paving.

6 Bed the paving on mortar, covering the edge of the liner. The paving should overlap the edge of the pool by about 3cm (1in). Finish off by pointing the joints with mortar using the mortaring trowel.

1 Mark out the shape of your pond with a piece of rope or garden hose or by sprinkling sand. If the pond is to be sited in a lawn, remove the turf by stripping off the grass to a depth of 5cm (2in) in squares of 30cm (12in) and stack upside-down in another part of the garden for later use.

2 Dig out the hole to a depth of 23cm (9in), angling the sides of the hole slightly inwards. By digging the sides at this slight angle there is less future risk of damage by expanding ice in severe winters and the sides are less likely to subside or crumble. The soil from the top 23cm (9in)

can be stored on a polythene (polyethylene) sheet nearby if it is likely to be used for any new contouring of the surrounds later. Rake the base of the hole to a rough level finish after the first layer of soil has been removed and mark with sand the position of any marginal shelves around the sides of the hole. These shelves should be 30cm (12in) wide and be positioned where you anticipate having the shallow water plants. The inner or deeper zone, avoiding the marginal shelf outlines, can now be dug out to the full depth of the pond, i.e. a further 23cm (9in) if the pond is to be 45cm (18in)

MAKING AN INFORMAL ROCK POOL

RIGHT: **Creeping thyme is a perfect carpeting plant for the dry soil where the pool edge is watertight.**

BELOW: **This is a good example of a rock edge, softened perfectly with *Caltha polypetala*.**

This informal pool uses the soil that was removed when the hole for the pool was excavated together with some pieces of rock in order to form the pool edge. The marginal plants grow in the wet soil behind the rocks, as do moisture-lovers further away from the water. Where the rock edge is made watertight, alpines can also be grown. The excavation process is the same as for an informal pool except that the marginal shelf is much wider to provide sufficient width for the rocks and for soil behind the rocks in which to plant marginals.

1 Mark out the shape of your pond with a length of rope or garden hose or by sprinkling sand. Stand back and view the shape from all angles to check that you are happy with the finished result.

2 Dig out the hole to a depth of 23–30cm (9–12in), angling the sides of the hole slightly inwards. By digging the sides at this slight angle there is less future risk of damage by expanding ice in severe winters and the sides are less likely to subside or crumble.

3 Rake the base of the hole to a rough level finish after the first layer of soil has been removed and mark with sand the position of any marginal shelves around the sides of the hole. These shelves should be 45cm (18in) wide and be positioned where you anticipate having the shallow water plants.

4 The inner or deeper zone, avoiding the marginal shelf outlines, can now be dug out to the full depth of the pond, i.e. a further 38cm (15in) for a 60cm (24in) deep pond. The soil from this deeper zone will be subsoil and can also be used later if positioned underneath any fresh topsoil. It should not become mixed with the freshly excavated topsoil. If you do not plan to use this subsoil later, then remove it from the site. Rake the

YOU WILL NEED

- Garden hose, rope or sand
- Spade
- Rake
- Spirit level
- Straight-edged piece of wood
- Underlay
- Flexible liner

- Bricks or heavy stones
- Rocks
- Ready-mixed mortar
- Cobbles
- Mortaring trowel
- Marginal and moisture-loving plants

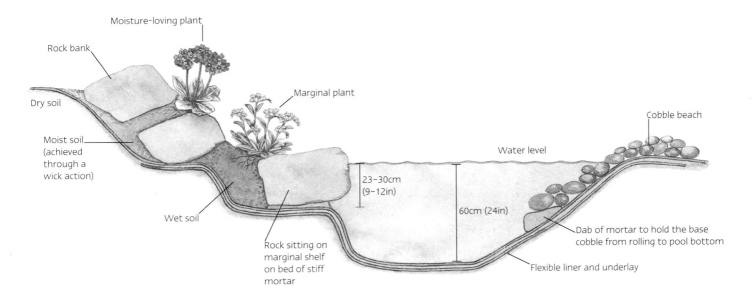

Moisture-loving plant

Rock bank

Dry soil

Moist soil (achieved through a wick action)

Marginal plant

Wet soil

Rock sitting on marginal shelf on bed of stiff mortar

Water level

23–30cm (9–12in)

60cm (24in)

Cobble beach

Dab of mortar to hold the base cobble from rolling to pool bottom

Flexible liner and underlay

bottom of the pond to achieve a level surface. A spirit level on a straight-edged piece of wood rested on the bottom will show levels.

5 Smooth over the surface of the pond by raking the bottom in order to remove any sharp stones or protruding surfaces. Go over the sides with your hands, removing any roots or sharp-edged objects. Gently firm the surface by patting.

6 Drape the underlay across the hole and the marginal shelves, leaving an overlap around the pool of about 30cm (12in).

7 If the flexible liner is small enough and help is available, it is much easier to unfold the liner away from the pool and then lift it in by the four corners. Take care not to disturb the underlay as the liner is lowered into place. Unfold a larger liner according to the supplier's directions.

8 Place weights, such as bricks or heavy stones, around the edges of the liner so that the wind does not blow the edges into the pool.

9 Lay the rocks on the liner on the inside edge of the marginal shelf, providing extra rigidity and protection for the liner with a bed of stiff mortar.

10 Once you are satisfied that the rocks are secure along the marginal shelves, backfill soil between the rocks and the edge of the flexible liner, making sure that the liner edge is always kept above the future water level.

11 The pool will look more natural if it is not completely surrounded by rocks and if a portion of the edge is made into a cobble beach. If you decide to include a cobble beach as part of the edging, there are a few points to bear in mind. To achieve a natural-looking effect, choose cobbles in a good range of sizes. Arrange the cobbles so that the main body of cobbles increases in diameter from below the waterline into the drier margins of the pond. In order to prevent the cobbles from rolling to the bottom of the pool, place a dab of stiff mortar on the flexible liner below the waterline, as is shown here. Alternatively, you can dig a small trench along the side of the pool and fill it with concrete to provide a support at the edge of the pool and lay the flexible liner over this (see page 67). Cut off any surplus liner around the pool.

12 Plant the marginals plants in the soil pockets between the rocks and fill the pond with water.

MAKING A WILDLIFE POOL

Having a large pool in order to attract a host of wildlife fascinates many people. The location of the pool is obviously one of the primary considerations. Siting the pool too close to the house will do nothing to encourage shy wildlife to approach the pool. If you are lucky enough to have a large garden, then you can easily situate a wildlife pool at the bottom of the garden, perhaps shielded from the house by shrubs or trees. This will make any wildlife feel more secure, and you will soon find that a range of insects, birds, amphibians and small mammals will become regular visitors.

ABOVE LEFT: The first priority in a wildlife pool is to create a small, shallow beach on part of the edge.

ABOVE RIGHT: This large informal pool will be a real magnet to wildlife in hot, arid weather.

RIGHT: The beach edge totally surrounds this wildlife pool with its pockets of informal foliage and colour.

1 Mark out the shape of the pool with a piece of rope or garden hose or by sprinkling sand. Choose a site close to some cover to encourage creatures to the edge.

2 Knock in pegs, approximately 2.5cm (1in) in diameter and 15cm (6in) long, at 1.8m (6ft) intervals and 15cm (6in) outside the outline. This will help you to establish an even level for the pond, which is a useful technique when you are working over a large area.

3 Fix one peg as the datum point for the finished water level of the pool. Using the spirit level and a straight-edged piece of wood, knock in the pegs so that the tops are level.

4 Any variations in level around the outline will become obvious once the pegs are level, allowing you to make adjustments to the surrounding soil.

5 Dig out the hole just inside the pegs to a depth of 75cm (30in) in a saucer shape, making the gradient on the sides shallow enough to retain soil without it slumping to the centre of the pool. Store the excavated soil on a polythene (polyethylene) sheet nearby as some of this soil will be required later.

YOU WILL NEED

- Garden hose, rope or sand
- Pegs, about 2.5cm (1in) in diameter and 15cm (6in) long
- Spirit level
- Straight-edged piece of wood
- Hammer
- Spade
- Large polythene (polyethylene) sheet
- Rake
- Underlay
- Flexible liner
- Bricks or heavy stones
- Washed, rounded cobbles
- Ready-mix mortar
- Flat rocks
- Plants (including bunches of oxygenators, deep-water aquatics and marginals)

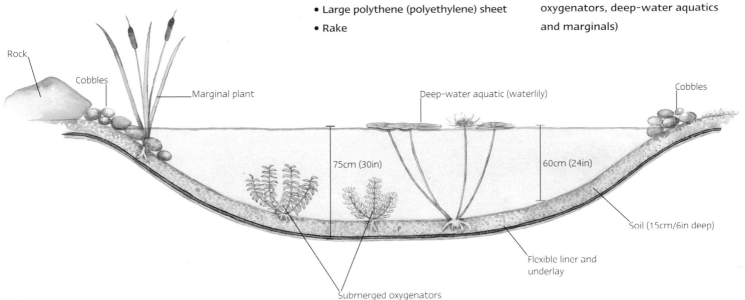

Rock

Cobbles

Marginal plant

Deep-water aquatic (waterlily)

Cobbles

75cm (30in)

60cm (24in)

Soil (15cm/6in deep)

Flexible liner and underlay

Submerged oxygenators

6 Rake the surface of the excavation to remove any sharp stones and exposed roots.

7 Drape the underlay across the hole, leaving an overlap of 8–15cm (3–6in) around the edge.

8 If the liner is large and heavy, follow the supplier's instructions on unfolding. This may involve placing the folded liner in the centre or at the end of the hole before unrolling a loose drape across the excavation. Make any adjustments to the liner by enlisting help to lift the four corners. Take care not to disturb the underlay as the liner is lifted and lowered into place.

9 Place weights, such as bricks or heavy stones, around the edge of the liner to prevent the wind blowing the edges into the pool.

10 Spread some of the topsoil removed earlier to a depth of 15cm (6in) over the liner.

11 At various points around the edge, create an edging of cobbles, ensuring that they will sit above and below the future water level. A dab of stiff mortar on the liner below the waterline into which the lower cobbles are bedded will stop the cobbles rolling

into the pond. Place large, flat rocks around the waterline for amphibians to hide beneath.

12 Before filling the pool, check that there is enough liner above the level pegs all the way around the pool outline. If the pool is large and it will be difficult to reach the centre, plant bunches of submerged oxygenators in the soil.

13 Pour in the water gently so as not to disturb the fresh, dry soil. Place a tile or flat rock just under the end of the garden hose to spread the flow as it trickles in.

14 As the water level rises, other plants can be put into the layer of soil just before the water reaches them.

15 Complete filling to within a few inches of the finished level so that any final adjustments to the sides can be made by adding or removing soil behind the edge of the liner. Remove the bricks holding the liner in place, along with the pegs. Finish the edges.

16 The water will be cloudy after filling. This is caused by fine soil particles escaping from the saturated soil. This will settle in a week or two, and should not be cured by a water change.

MAKING A BOG AREA
with an independent liner

Most informal water gardens would look incomplete without the companion plants in the moist or wet soil near the water. Such an area not only increases the variety of plants, but also makes the pool appear more natural. The wide range of species that can be grown in these conditions is one of the many bonuses of having an informal pool. Using a liner to create a bog garden is one of the simplest and cheapest ways of creating a permanently moist environment that will allow these plants to achieve their potential.

An independent bog garden is much more satisfactory than one that has been created by extending the liner that is used

for the pool. Plants in a bog garden tend to have lush foliage and as a result make high demands on soil moisture. Where the bog garden is linked to the pool, the wick effect of moisture from the pool to the bog will lead to a fall in the water level, which can be considerable in hot, sunny weather. A separate bog garden can be managed independently of the pool, and it is also possible to add fertilizers to the soil in the bog garden without any danger of upsetting the balance of the chemistry in the pool water. The siting and design can be so organized that the bog garden appears to be a natural extension or a separate feature.

Because the waterproofing material used to line the bog garden is completely covered with soil and is pierced at the bottom, there is no need to use expensive, ultra-violet-resistant liners. Heavy-duty polythene (polyethylene) of the kind sold by builders' merchants is perfectly adequate. The liner must be pierced so that the wet soil drains slowly or it will become completely stagnant and anaerobic, but this slow seepage of water through the bottom means that a whole range of moisture-loving plants that would not survive in a saturated soil can be grown as well as several marginals that will thrive in the damp conditions.

YOU WILL NEED

- String or sand
- Spade
- Polythene (polyethylene) sheets
- Rake
- Bricks or stones
- Garden fork
- Flexible plastic pipe, 2.5cm (1in) in diameter
- Small electric drill
- Wooden bung
- Screw
- Pea shingle or gravel
- Timber to tamp the backfill
- Garden hose and connector fitting
- 1 elbow joint
- Rigid plastic pipe, 2.5cm (1in) in diameter

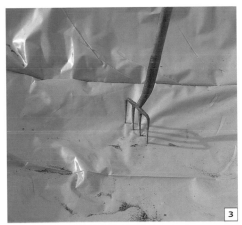

1 Mark out a suitable shape with string or sand, then dig a hole about 40cm (16in) deep with slightly sloping sides to minimize crumbling on light sandy soils. Store the topsoil you have removed on a polythene (polyethylene) sheet nearby because you will use it later to fill the hole. Rake the sides and the bottom of the hole smooth.

2 Drape a sheet of polythene (polyethylene) into the hole and mould it roughly into the outline. Use bricks or stones to hold the sheet of polythene in place around the edges so that it does not blow away.

3 Use a garden fork to pierce the liner in one or two places to allow water to seep slowly away from the bog. On a light sandy soil in areas of low rainfall, only one or two piercings will be necessary. If the surrounding soil is heavy clay, then you will need to pierce every metre (3ft).

4 Pierce a flexible plastic pipe at 15cm (6in) intervals with small holes. As these tend to become blocked easily, use a small drill to ensure the holes are large enough.

5 Insert a bung into one end of the pipe. This can be made from a piece of old broom handle. Secure the bung by drilling a screw through the pipe into the bung.

6 Spread pea shingle or gravel across the bottom of the hole to a depth of 5cm (2in). Lay the flexible pipe across the shingle so that it protrudes slightly above ground. Spread a further layer of pea shingle, 5cm (2in) thick, across the pipe and rake level.

7 Replace the topsoil, which has been stored at the side of the hole, until it reaches the original soil level, and tamp it down to consolidate it. Any surplus liner sticking out of the ground can be trimmed off and the surplus soil disposed of.

8 Attach a garden hose with a hose-connector fitting to the plastic pipe sticking out of the ground. Plant up the bed and nourish the planting by watering the bog area until the water appears on the surface. Disconnect the hose and connect the flexible pipe by an elbow joint to a rigid, upright section of pipe and use this to top up the bed every week in dry weather.

MAKING A DRIED RIVER BED

Gravel gardens are becoming increasingly popular, and are more convincing if they have a definite theme, such as a dried river bed. This is simple to construct in that it places no demands on levels and waterproofing, yet, when successfully designed, it has a distinctly watery theme. It helps if the width of the river bed varies from one end to the other, and, if there is a slight slope in the garden, this looks even more effective with the narrow origin of the river bed at the top of the slope. On a totally flat site, introduce a slight curve to simulate the meandering line which a river would take on low-lying, flat land. It can look most appropriate in a long or narrow garden where the viewing point from the house allows the length of the river bed to be framed in a downstairs window.

As with all gravel gardens, there is a greater freedom in the planting arrangements compared with having to work within the disciplined confines of a border.

Access to individual plants or plant groups is possible from all sides, and even after heavy rain you will not encounter the associated problems of picking up mud or compacting the wet soil by walking on it.

BELOW: **The origin of this dried river bed appears from a thick shrub border and is sparsely planted, initially with a selection of drought-loving plants.**

INSET: **As the bed becomes wider in the lower section, moisture-loving grasses are introduced and allowed to grow through an old bottomless boat for a further watery effect.**

YOU WILL NEED

- Garden hose, rope or sand
- Spade
- Rake
- Landscape membrane
- Large scissors

- Squares of polythene (polyethylene)
- Small pea gravel or shingle
- Rounded pebbles or cobbles

- Planting compost (soil mix)
- Plants (including moisture-lovers)
- Watering can
- Large boulders

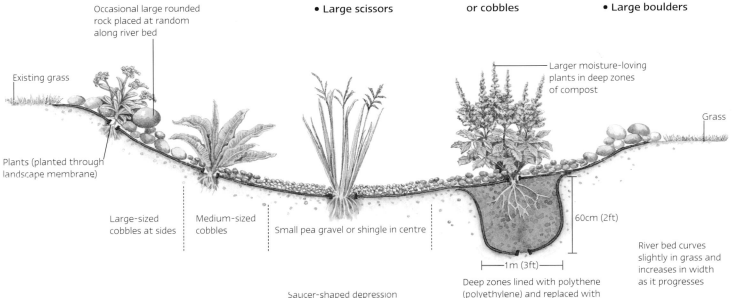

Occasional large rounded rock placed at random along river bed

Existing grass

Larger moisture-loving plants in deep zones of compost

Grass

Plants (planted through landscape membrane)

Large-sized cobbles at sides

Medium-sized cobbles

Small pea gravel or shingle in centre

60cm (2ft)

1m (3ft)

River bed curves slightly in grass and increases in width as it progresses

Saucer-shaped depression no deeper than 15–23cm (6–9in)

Deep zones lined with polythene (polyethylene) and replaced with humus-rich compost (soil mix) after digging out

1 Mark out the shape of the bed with a thin line of sand or with a length of rope or garden hose laid on the ground. View the shape from all angles, particularly from any upstairs windows.

2 If the proposed site is on existing turf, remove the turf to a depth of 2.5cm (1in), and stack somewhere inconspicuous for later use or remove from the site.

3 Create a shallow, evenly sloped, saucer-shaped depression across the width of the river bed along its length. The depth of the base of the saucer need be no more than 15–23cm (6–9in), depending on the width of the bed. Rake smooth and remove any sharp objects.

4 If moisture-loving plants are to be included in the bed, mark their positions and dig out large planting holes, about 60cm (2ft) deep and 1m (3ft) in diameter.

5 Line the whole river bed with a landscape membrane, which allows moisture through, but prevents the growth of weeds. These materials are often sold in 1m- (3ft-) wide rolls.

6 If planting holes have been dug out beforehand, cut out holes in the membrane above the planting positions and line the holes with squares of polythene (polyethylene), piercing the base with a hole.

7 Cover the whole area of the river bed with small pea gravel or shingle and 2–3 grades of rounded pebbles or cobbles, using the larger sizes on the outside and the smaller sizes in the centre.

8 Plant into the bed where desired by scraping back the cobbles and cutting a cross in the membrane. Fold back the flaps of cut membrane and remove enough soil from underneath to allow the plant roots to be spread out in the planting hole with supplementary planting compost (soil mix).

9 Water the new plants thoroughly before covering the compost (soil mix) with the folds of membrane. Push back the pebbles over the planting position.

10 For the moisture-loving plants in the specially dug larger planting holes, place some of the removed turf from the earlier preparation of the river bed in the bottom of the holes before inserting the planting compost (soil mix). The turf helps to retain more compost in the planting holes before any surplus can seep out through the hole pierced earlier in the polythene (polyethylene) lining.

11 Add larger boulders onto the river bed to add interest between the plants.

INSTALLING A PREFORMED UNIT

If you choose a preformed unit, do not be tempted to skimp on the preparation of the hole and make sure that the sides and base are evenly supported. The larger units are extremely heavy when full of water and are subject to enormous strain if they are not properly supported. This can result in hairline cracks forming in even the thicker fibreglass units. Greater care is necessary with the plastic preformed units because their sides are less rigid and can bend in any uneven pressure of water and soil.

YOU WILL NEED

- Preformed pool unit
- Bricks
- Canes and a garden hose, rope or string
- Spade
- Rake
- 2 pieces of straight-edged wood: one long enough to straddle the sides of the pool unit and the other slightly shorter than the length of the pool in order to check the level at the bottom of the hole
- Tape measure
- Spirit level
- Knife or secateurs (pruners)
- Soft sand
- Timber for tamping the backfill
- Suitable edging material such as paving slabs to create an informal edge

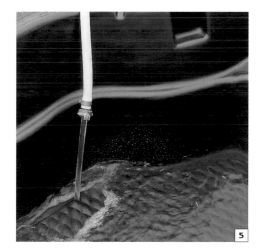

3 You will need some help to place the unit in the hole and press it down firmly onto the raked surface so that an impression is made of the shape of the base. Lift out the unit, then dig out from 5–8cm (2–3in) outside the impression that has been left by the unit's base. When the depth of the pool plus an extra 5–8cm (2–3in) for a layer of soft sand has been reached, lay a plank of wood across the width of the hole and check that the hole is the right depth with a tape measure. Use a spirit level to make sure that the base of the hole is level.

4 Cut away any tree roots that may have been exposed and rake over the bottom to remove stones and any other objects with a sharp edge. Check the sides for sharp edges with your hands, gently patting firm any loose soil. Firm the base evenly before spreading a layer of soft sand, 5cm (2in) deep, across the bottom. Again, get help to lower the unit carefully into place. Make sure that the unit is sitting level by placing the spirit level on a straight-edged piece of wood across the sides; check the level in all directions.

5 Gently add water to the unit to a depth of 10cm (4in) and fill between the sides of the unit and the sides of the hole with sand or sifted soil to a depth of 10cm (4in) from the bottom, so that it is equal to the level of the water in the pool. Use a flat-bottomed piece of timber – a cut-down broom handle, for example – to firm this backfilled sand or soil into place.

6 Repeat the process of adding 10cm (4in) of water to the pool and 10cm (4in) of sand or soil outside, making sure that no air pockets are left as you backfill around the pool. Use your spirit level to check that the unit is still perfectly level after each addition of water and sand. When the pool is nearly full, the weight of the water will keep it quite stable. The edging can then be put in place. Crazy paving makes an excellent choice for informal edges, covering the rim of the pool and just overlapping the water.

1 To mark out a symmetrically shaped preformed pool, invert the unit onto the proposed site and use sand to mark around the edge of the rim. An irregularly shaped unit should be stood upright on the proposed site and temporarily supported by bricks to prevent it from falling over. The outline can then be marked by pushing canes from the rim into the soil directly beneath, at intervals of about 1m (3ft). A garden hose, rope or string can then be placed around the canes to mark the outline on the ground.

2 Skim off the turf in 30cm (12in) squares and stack them where they can rot down. Excavate the soil down to the level of the first marginal shelf, working from 5–8cm (2–3in) outside the outline. Lightly rake and level the dug surface.

CREATING A CLAY-LINED POOL

BELOW: **Large informal pools are ideal candidates for lining with clay. This pool will be attractive to wildlife. A small, thatched summer-house provides a perfect vantage point from which to view visiting creatures.**

The introduction of flexible liners has meant that clay, like concrete, is no longer a common method of pool construction. It can, however, be a good proposition if there is already heavy clay on site or if it can be bought cheaply from a local source. Making a clay-lined pool is not a viable economic undertaking for a small pool if the clay has to be imported from some distance away. It is not completely waterproof, and the very slow absorption of water through its sides makes it more appropriate for large pools and wildlife pools in rural areas.

Few garden soils are composed entirely of clay and in order to check whether the soil in your garden contains sufficient clay to make a puddled pool, there are two simple tests. The first and easiest is to roll a sample between the palms. If it falls to pieces it is unsuitable. It should stay tacky when moist and stain the skin as it rolls.

A more accurate test requires placing a sifted sample in a jar of water to which a teaspoon of salt is added. Shake it vigorously and leave it for a day or two. It will settle into bands of sand, silt and clay from the bottom upwards. If it is suitable for pool making, at least two-thirds of the sample should be clay, which forms the top layer.

The process of clay puddling means lining a hole with a thick, compacted layer of clay, preferably in several thin layers. It should be at least 15–25cm (6–10in) thick, so work out the area of the base and sides first to find out the quantity you need.

If you do not have a ready supply of natural clay or cannot obtain it locally, you can instead use sodium bentonite clay and bentomat matting, which is much easier to install and will generally achieve better results.

YOU WILL NEED

- String, sand or canes
- Spade
- Rolls of bentomat matting
- Bag of sodium bentonite crystals
- Plants (including oxygenating plants and marginals)
- Garden hose
- Tile or stone slab

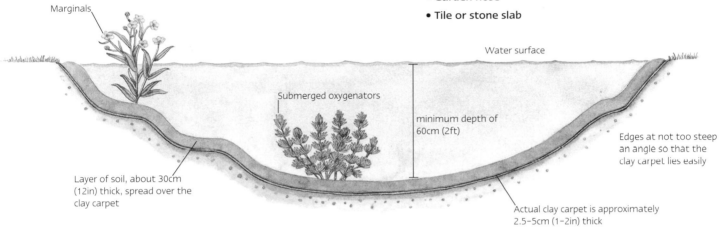

Marginals

Water surface

Submerged oxygenators

minimum depth of 60cm (2ft)

Edges at not too steep an angle so that the clay carpet lies easily

Layer of soil, about 30cm (12in) thick, spread over the clay carpet

Actual clay carpet is approximately 2.5–5cm (1–2in) thick

RIGHT: This natural pool in a shaded site, with its inky black water, is lined with clay. This allows the moisture-loving plants greater freedom around the edge, which is kept moist.

LEFT: Tree roots can be a menace in clay-lined pools where there is a very low water table. Here, the water table is fed by a spring, keeping the water table high and allowing ample water for the tree roots.

1 Mark out the position of the pool on the ground with string or sand or with a series of canes.

2 Excavate a saucer-shaped depression to a minimum of 60cm (2ft) at the deepest point. Avoid creating steep sides to the hole. Save the topsoil for replacing on the clay carpet later.

3 Roll the bentomat over the excavation and over the edges. Overlap any additional strips by about 15cm (6in), sprinkling loose bentonite crystals between and over the joints to strengthen the seal.

4 Cover the bentomat with a 30cm (12in) layer of soil, avoiding soil which contains heavy levels of fertilizer.

5 Suitable marginals and oxygenating plants can be planted directly into the soil. Avoid using very vigorous marginals, such as *Typha*, *Sparganium* and *Schoenoplectus*, and instead choose less vigorous types – *Caltha*, *Veronica* and *Myosotis*, for example.

6 Add water by resting the end of the garden hose on a tile or stone slab and letting the water in slowly. This prevents the freshly installed soil from being dislodged. The fine particles of debris, silt and clay may take several days or weeks to settle on the bottom, but the water will then begin to clear.

MAKING A CONCRETE POOL

RIGHT: **A shallow pool, which acts as a base pool for a fountain, is made from concrete blocks skimmed on the inside with a waterproof mortar.**

BELOW: **A concrete block wall provides strength and water-proofing inside the dry wall surround of this pool, which is disguised by the natural walling stones.**

Before the widespread use of flexible liners, concrete was the only material used for ornamental pool construction. It often involved complicated shuttering (formwork) to make a framework into which fresh concrete was poured. Although modern materials have largely superseded concrete in pool construction, there are still situations in which concrete pools are more suitable, such as places where soil conditions are too unstable for sunken pools with flexible liners. Concrete is also good for raised pools, which need strong side walls to withstand water pressure. Fish-keepers also use concrete pools, as the rigid vertical side walls necessary for pools with large specimen fish are more suited to concrete construction. Instead of using wooden shuttering and pouring wet concrete into the moulds, most concrete pools are now made using concrete walling blocks to make the rigid framework and this is then skimmed with fibreglass mortar to make it watertight.

YOU WILL NEED

- String and canes
- Spade
- Concrete mix for walling block foundations
- Spirit level
- Straight-edged piece of wood
- Rake
- Soft sand

- Reinforcing fibres
- Ready-mix mortar
- Plasterer's trowel
- Concrete walling blocks
- Hardcore
- Paving slabs as surround
- Paint brush
- Black waterproof sealant

Paving surround

Water level

Hardcore

Concrete walling block

Soil

Layer of mortar, 1cm (½in) thick, over the walls and base with reinforcing fibres in the mix

Concrete infill between walling blocks and sides of excavation

Concrete foundation, 20cm (8in) wide and 6cm (2½in) deep

Layer of mortar, 1cm (½in) thick, with reinforcing fibres in the mix

Layer of soft sand, 5cm (2in) thick

1 Mark out the outline of the pool with string and canes, making a nick in the soil along the outline.

2 Dig out the area to a depth of 75cm (30in). If you are keeping the soil, do not mix topsoil and subsoil.

3 Dig a 20cm- (8in-) wide trench to a depth of 6cm (2½in) around the inside of the base of the excavation for the concrete wall foundations. Pour in the concrete mix and level the top of the foundation. Check that the foundations are level using a spirit level on a piece of wood, and leave to dry for 24 hours.

4 Dig out about 6cm (2½in) soil from the base of the pool and rake to remove any stones. Spread and rake, then level and firm a 5cm (2in) layer of soft sand so that it is just below the top of the wall foundation.

5 As the base of the pool is well supported by the soil beneath the sand, all that is necessary is to skim the sand with a 1cm (½in) layer of fibre-reinforced mortar with a plasterer's trowel, overlapping the concrete foundations by 5cm (2in).

6 After a minimum of 24 hours, concrete walling blocks are then mortared onto the foundations and

the levels checked with a spirit level. After the mortar has set, give added strength to the walls by filling in the gap between the soil wall and the walling blocks with a stiff concrete mix. Fill in the inside of the blocks if these have been made with internal cavities.

7 Allow a further 48 hours for the whole structure to set thoroughly. Dampen the whole surface of the internal structure, including the base, before covering with a 1cm (½in) layer of fibre-reinforced mortar. To give the corners added strength, make a rounded cornice edge where the walls meet each other and the base.

8 Replace the top 10cm (4in) of soil with hardcore to help form a secure base immediately around the pool. Mortar the paving edge onto the walls of the pool and the hardcore base. Place the paving surround so that it overlaps the inside wall of the pool by 2.5–5cm (1–2in).

9 Allow the internal walls to dry for a further 48 hours, then paint them with a black waterproof sealant. This will also prevent any impurities from the mortar from seeping into the water.

BUILDING AN ORNAMENTAL POOL
for fish

Specialist fish-keepers tend to prefer raised pools if possible, particularly collectors of large specimen koi. Apart from being able to see them easily, it is useful to have vertical side walls both below and slightly above the water surface to prevent them leaping out onto the surrounding paving. The practicalities of pool hygiene and management for large fish call for more attention to the design and construction than the average pool.

For the ornamental garden pool a good compromise can be found in building a more traditional sunken pool and adding filtration. The more formal designs have the advantage of paved edges which, provided they have a slight overhang above the water surface, will help to stop the fish's tendency to jump out. An external filter can be more difficult to disguise in a formal pool and one of the more aesthetic ways of hiding a large external filter is to build a raised waterfall alongside the pool where the filter can be positioned above the pond level. The black box-like filter can then be disguised by the planting around and behind the waterfall. Where external filtration is not possible there are large internal pond filters which can be used, although they are not as easy to clean and maintain as an external filter.

RIGHT: **The quantity of fish in this small pool is dependent on the extra oxygen supplied by a waterfall and a hidden filtration system which prevents the water becoming toxic.**

YOU WILL NEED

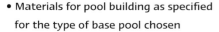

- Materials for pool building as specified
  for the type of base pool chosen
- Materials for stream building as specified
  for the type of stream chosen
- Biological filter
- Ultra-violet clarifier
- Submersible filter pump
- Flexible delivery pipe and hacksaw
  for cutting to appropriate lengths
- Galvanized hose clips
- Magnet attachment to reduce blanketweed
- Flat rock to disguise end of pipe

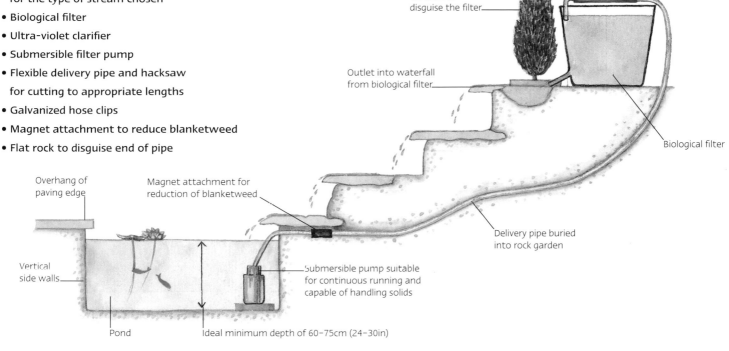

Outlet from
ultra-violet
clarifier into
biological filter

Delivery pipe enters
ultra-violet clarifier
before entering
biological filter

Conifers to
disguise the filter

Outlet into waterfall
from biological filter

Biological filter

Overhang of
paving edge

Magnet attachment for
reduction of blanketweed

Delivery pipe buried
into rock garden

Vertical
side walls

Submersible pump suitable
for continuous running and
capable of handling solids

Pond

Ideal minimum depth of 60–75cm (24–30in)

1 Following the instructions given previously, build a pool, either from concrete or with a flexible liner, which has an adequate volume for a collection of ornamental fish. A preformed unit pool could also act as a fish pool although the size may limit the numbers that can be kept. The three necessities for making a pool suitable for fish are a minimum depth of 60–75cm (24–30in), no shallow sloping sides, such as beaches, where larger fish may flip out, and an overhang of 2.5–5cm (1–2in) if any paved edge is used.

2 Follow the instructions for making a stream with rigid stream units or a flexible liner.

3 The following steps show how to set up a filtration system in a pool for fish. The two main ingredients for a fish pool are a biological filter and an ultra-violet clarifier, which need a mains electricity supply. Work out the volume of the pool, and consult a dealer regarding the size of filter and clarifier you will need. There are various designs for the interior of a biological filter and several filter mediums may be used. The dealer will supply the most suitable filter medium for your needs.

4 Position the filter behind or to the side of the top stream section or header pool so that the outlet from the filter will be piped into the stream. Place the filter, which measures about 60cm (24in) wide and 60cm (24in) deep, slightly higher than the top of the stream and in a position that allows the planting to hide it.

5 The filter pump should be suitable for continuous running and for handling solids. If it is too small, the filtration will be inadequate; if it is too large, it will change the water too often. The volume of the pool should not pass through the filter more than once an hour.

6 Hide the delivery pipe from the pump in the soil alongside the stream and connect it to the ultra-violet clarifier at the top of the stream with a galvanized hose clip. Use another short length of pipe to connect the outlet of the clarifier to the inlet of the biological filter with hose clips. Fix the magnet attachment to the pipe where it runs under the first fall above the pond.

7 Finally, connect a short length of pipe from the outlet of the filter to the header pool or top stream section, disguising the end of the pipe with a flat rock where it enters the stream. Fill the base pool with water and turn on the system. Run it continuously for a few weeks to allow the bacteria to grow on the media and begin to work. Once the system is working after a few weeks, keep the pump operating as the beneficial bacteria will die if water is not passing through for any length of time.

BUILDING A RAISED POOL

YOU WILL NEED

- String, rope, pegs or sand
- Preformed pool unit
- Spade
- Rake
- Gravel
- Railway sleepers (ties)
- Builder's square
- Electric saw
- Sand and sieved soil
- Galvanized steel brackets
- Screws and screwdriver
- Nails and hammer
- Polythene (polyethylene) sheet
- Spirit level
- Straight-edged piece of wood
- Timber for tamping the backfill
- Small rocks
- Creeping and mat-forming alpines
- Alpine grit

Raised pools are easier to empty than sunken pools, and they suffer from fewer problems, such as leaves and other plant debris blowing in. They require very little excavation and are an ideal solution on sloping sites. Substantial surrounds, such as twin walls, are necessary when a raised pool is made with a flexible liner in order to withstand the internal water pressure, and this makes them more costly to build than sunken pools; if they are built with brick or walling stone, some degree of bricklaying skill will be necessary.

A simple raised pool can be made by installing a rigid preformed unit and surrounding it with a raised edge of several courses of old railway sleepers (ties), secured with brackets. Alternatively, a rigid unit can be raised above the ground according to the height and type of rock edging.

INITIAL PREPARATION

Mark the outline of the shape that the raised wall of railway sleepers (ties) will occupy. Check that the preformed unit will fit inside the outline. Clear the turf and other plants from the ground beneath the position of the pool and rake the soil level. Spread a layer of gravel, 5cm (2in) deep, over the marked-out area. This will prevent the bottom course of sleepers from sitting on wet soil.

1 After marking out and preparing a level site, lay the first course of sleepers to the shape required. For a simple rectangle, which will hold a variety of preformed shapes, you will need to cut down half of the sleepers to form the two shorter sides and use a builder's square to check that a true right angle is formed by the sleepers on the short side. A square surround with sides that are the same length will save considerable cutting. Whenever possible, butt a freshly cut edge to the inside of a neighbouring sleeper so that it is not exposed.

2 As the courses are placed on top of each other, place the next course of sleepers (ties) in a different pattern. Extra rigidity in the construction is then provided by bonding the joints. Continue adding courses until the correct level of the preformed unit is reached. If this is not the exact height of the preform, add another sleeper so that the wall is higher than the pool.

3 When sufficient height is reached (in this case the height of four sleepers/ties), spread a 5cm (2in) layer of sand inside the surround to act as a base for the preform. This will make any final levelling of the rigid unit much easier.

4 Make the structure more rigid by screwing a galvanized steel bracket inside the corners of the surround to connect each sleeper (tie) to the next.

5 Extra rigidity will be given by driving in galvanized nails, 15cm (6in) long, from one course of sleepers (ties) to the next. Knock the nails in at an angle on the inside edge of the surround so that they are not seen later.

6 Line the inside of the raised bed with a sheet of cheap polythene (polyethylene) secured to the sleepers (ties) by nails. This helps to prevent small mammals like mice from creeping inside the gaps between the sleepers and making nests in the soil or sand.

7 Enlist help to lift the pool inside the sleepers (ties) and check that the sides are level. Keep the sides of the pool just lower than the top of the sleeper wall.

8 Add sieved soil between the pool rim and the sleepers (ties). Firm this with a ramming tool like a sawn-off broom handle and then level the backfilled soil around the rim. The area between the edge of the pool and the sleepers can now be landscaped with small rocks and a selection of alpine plants, top-dressed with alpine grit.

5

6

7

8

BUILDING A STREAM
with a flexible liner

YOU WILL NEED

- Marking pegs, string, rope or sand
- Spade
- Rake
- Soft sand
- Underlay and flexible liner
- Corrugated delivery pipe
- Large, flat-sided spillstone
- Ready-mixed mortar
- Mortaring trowel
- Rocks
- Submersible pump
- Hose connectors
- Flow-regulating valve
- Cobbles

This stream has been constructed using one sheet of flexible liner because there are no sharp changes of direction. The size of liner is calculated by placing a tape measure loosely along the proposed line of the stream and adding extra length for the height and number of vertical falls. Additional length should also be anticipated in the overlap into the base pool, and the folds made in the liner. Finally, in measuring the length, allow additional liner for the depth of the header pool. The width should be measured as the maximum width of the stream, even if this is for only one section. The header pool is likely to be the widest part of the watercourse and by adding twice the depth of this pool to its width, you will be able to measure the exact width of liner needed and buy it in one sheet.

It can be difficult to assess accurately the size of pump required to use with a stream, and advice should be sought from the supplier. It is always better to err on the side of over capacity rather than buy a pump that has to work hard to maintain the volume of water over the waterfalls.

Check that the diameter of the delivery pipe is suitable for the outlet of the pump. To feed a reasonable length of stream – say 4m (13ft) – the pipe should be preferably 2.5cm (1in) in diameter.

1 Mark out the route of the watercourse with pegs and string or rope or by sprinkling sand. Decide on the position of the waterfalls because the stream will have to narrow to waists at these falls. A stream with falls is a series of narrow, level pools at different heights. By making these pools level, water is retained in each section when the pump is turned on. If the sections slope towards the base pool, the stream would dry up as soon as the pump is switched off.

2 Begin to excavate at the edge of the existing base pool which is made with a preformed unit. This is the point where suitable stones will form the outlet into the pool. The gradient of the slope and the size of the rocks will govern the height of the waterfalls. Dig out and rake a flat-bottomed trench, 23cm (9in) deep, from the base pool to the point where there will be a waterfall from the header pool. This is excavated at the top of the stream. Line the trench with a 2.5cm (1in) covering of soft sand, then the underlay and liner can be unrolled into the excavation. Allow the liner to rest on the marginal shelf and unroll it along the

stream to just beyond the outlet waterfall. Ensure the liner and underlay are placed correctly over the excavation, and that there will be enough to overlap the sides of the stream once it is pressed into the contours. Bury the delivery pipe beside the stream; it should reach from the bottom of the base pool to beyond the header pool.

3 Select a large stone with flat sides as the spillstone for the outlet waterfall into the base pool. The stone should be placed on a stiff dab of mortar on top of the stream liner and positioned so that it overhangs the side of the base pool.

4 Place rocks along the stream edge on top of the liner, ensuring that they are higher than the top of the spillstone into the base pool. Soil can later be placed between the liner and the rocks for creeping marginals in the wet soil (see inset).

5 At the top of the stream, place a stone in the centre of the liner, over which the water will flow from the header pool into the stream. To prevent the water seeping under this spillstone, fold the liner behind the stone and place smaller rocks behind and to the sides.

6 As the supporting walls for the waterfall are built up, mortar these into place behind and around the spillstone, ensuring that the small pleat in the liner is hidden between rocks and covered with mortar. Make sure that the side stones flanking the spillstone finish at a higher level so that the water is channelled over the spillstone.

7 Bring the end of the delivery pipe to the surface above the rocks behind the header pool. Use a flat stone to conceal the pipe where it enters the header pool. Keep the end of the pipe above the waterline in case it siphons the water back into the base pool when the pump is turned off.

8 Fill the base pool with water, attach the pump and valve to the pipe, and turn on to test the flow of water. Add some soil around the rocks beside the stream and plant a mixture of moisture-lovers and alpines. Disguise the folds of the liner on the stream bottom with rounded cobbles.

BUILDING A STREAM
with rigid units

YOU WILL NEED

- Plastic dustbin (trash can)
- Length of corrugated flexible pipe
- Roof tiles
- Submersible pump
- 2 bricks or a piece of broken paving
- Timber for tamping the backfill
- Galvanized metal mesh
- Cobbles
- Preformed stream units
- Small stakes or pegs and tape measure
- Spade
- Soft sand
- Spirit level
- Straight-edged piece of wood
- Bucket
- Flow-adjusting valve

You may prefer to use rigid, preformed stream units instead of a flexible liner to build a stream. These eliminate the need for mortar and require very little skill to install. Installation is much quicker than with liners, largely because you do not have to wait for mortar to harden, and the units can be easily removed if necessary.

The strongest stream units are those made from fibreglass. They are resistant to ultra-violet light and strong enough to withstand a certain amount of movement in the soil mound. The vacuum-formed plastic types have a limited life expectancy and are much more easily damaged. Most types are available in a variety of finishes, such as pebbledash or textured rock.

Because streams are best created with a header pool at the water's point of origin in the system, check that you can also get a suitable pool in the same finish as the stream units. These pools must contain sufficient water to ensure that when the pump is not running there is no surge of water when the flow is turned on.

Unlike streams made with a flexible liner, there is no moist edge in the soil immediately surrounding the units, and this dry soil is not suitable for marginal and moisture-loving plants. There are, however, several creeping plants, such as *Acaena*, *Arenaria* and *Erigeron*, that will grow in these dry conditions and quickly disguise the rather artificial edges of the units.

1 This stream runs into a submerged reservoir rather than a pool, so dig a plastic dustbin (trash can) into the ground where the stream ends. Mound up the spoil from the excavation and some extra soil in a gentle slope along the route of the proposed stream. Bury a length of flexible pipe, which forms the delivery pipe from the pump, along the length of the stream to reappear above the surface at the top of the stream. Here, the pipe was taken through a low wall when it was constructed. Protect the pipe by covering it with roof tiles before replacing the soil. Use a pipe with a minimum diameter of 2.5cm (1in) if the distance from the reservoir to the top of the stream is more than 3m (10ft).

2 Place the pump on a piece of broken paving at the bottom of the reservoir to keep the pump intake just above any sludge which might accumulate at the bottom of the reservoir. Connect the pump cable to the nearby connection point and connect the plastic pipe to the pump outlet. Measure the

length of the stream between the reservoir and the top and select the required number of stream sections. There are different lengths available so buy the sections first before marking out the stream outline.

3 Backfill the soil and firm around the rim of the reservoir before placing a piece of galvanized metal mesh over the top. Place a few cobbles on the mesh to hold it in place until the preformed units are finally installed.

4 Lay the stream units down roughly on the ground to design a route. Vary the direction as much as possible; it is much easier to do this with preformed units than with flexible liners. Mark out their positions with small stakes or pegs.

5 Remove the units and, starting at the bottom, dig a shallow trench for the units and line it with a layer of soft sand. Press the first two sections firmly into a level position with the outlet of the bottom section projecting over the reservoir by 7-10cm (3-4in). As the units are designed to hold a thin film of shallow water when they are level, pour in some water to check the final level and flow over the rim.

6 The stream units are designed to overlap one another and produce a gentle cascade even with a small pump. This flow is achieved with the bucket and will be increased when the pump is turned on.

7 Once the final section has been installed at the top of the stream, add some water to check the position and levels. Backfill the soil around the sides in order to blend the edges of the units into the mound. To disguise the side of the top stream section, mound cobbles on top of the wall and around the stream source. Use more cobbles to blend the sections into the surrounding mound of soil.

8 To adjust the flow of water over the cobbles, insert a plastic flow-adjusting valve into the flexible pipe at a convenient point near the top of the stream. Fill the reservoir, then turn on the pump to check that the stream is flowing satisfactorily. Finish arranging cobbles over the metal grid.

INSTALLING A BRIMMING URN

YOU WILL NEED

- Underlay and a piece of old carpet
- Spare pieces of flexible liner
- Bricks or decorative walling blocks
- Ready-mix mortar or
  brick or stone adhesive
- Galvanized metal grid or mesh
- Wire cutters
- Plastic-coated wire
- Submersible pump
- Urn
- Electric drill with a suitable bit
- Water-tank coupler or waterproof
  sealant with rigid delivery pipe
- Flexible delivery pipe or plastic pipe
- Hose clip
- Copper pipe, 10mm (½in) in diameter
- Cobbles and stones

Reservoir features, which can be used to create focal points in the garden, require minimal maintenance, and the relatively simple construction techniques involved can be applied to a range of features, including large urns. As with a drilled rock fountain, where the water trickles, rather than gurgles, from the top, the brimming urn can be an attractive proposition to the garden owner who wants to introduce the movement of water without any noise. In more formal types of garden, too, an urn can be used to make a stronger statement than other smaller fountain features.

Most urns are made of terracotta, and you must check that your urn will be frost resistant if it is to remain outside all winter. If there is the slightest doubt about its frost-hardiness, the urn should be painted with one of the proprietary water sealing paints that are recommended for outdoor use for sealing brick walls or other absorbent surfaces.

If you are using a brand new urn, paint it as soon as you obtain it, because terracotta is likely to be completely dry at this stage. If you are converting an existing urn that has been outside in a moist climate for some time or has been used to contain plants, dry it as much as you can before painting. If you do not, the moisture will be locked into the terracotta and could cause it to crack if there are any severe fluctuations in temperature. Apply three coats of paint both inside and out, allowing each coat ample time to dry thoroughly before applying the next. One advantage of the sealant on the outside surface is that the water will flow much more evenly than on the raw terracotta. The water flow is also helped if the rim is level, so if you are buying a new one, choose a suitably rimmed style.

The urn can be sited as a free-standing feature in a border or on paving or gravel. Or, it may form a strong focal point in the centre of an existing pool. If it is to be free-standing, the method of installation is the same as for installing a millstone fountain, except for the details given opposite for inserting the delivery pipe into the urn. The steps on the opposite page describe how an urn can be installed in a raised flowerbed or soil border.

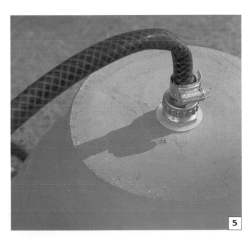

1 A good site for a brimming urn is in a small garden where there is a paved or concrete base which would be difficult to break up in order to sink a reservoir. This pool will create an adequately sized reservoir which will not require frequent topping up. Remove the plants from the centre of the bed, but leave some of the perennials to soften the edges. Remove most of the soil.

2 Place a square of old carpet or underlay at the bottom of the hole to protect the liner. Drape the liner in the hole and build up a pier of bricks in the centre until it is level with the top of the bed. Bond the bricks together for extra strength with ready-mix mortar or a brick or stone adhesive.

3 Place a sheet of galvanized metal grid over the hole. The sheet should be large enough to be supported by the sides of the hole and the brick pier in the centre. Cut a square in the grid large enough for the pump to pass through and secure with plastic-coated wire to form a hinge.

4 Place the pump in the bottom of the reservoir by passing it through the small access square next to the brick pier.

5 Drill a hole in the bottom of the urn large enough to accept a 10mm ($\frac{1}{2}$in) water-tank coupler. If it is not possible to obtain a water-tank coupler, a rigid delivery pipe from the pump can be passed through the base hole, made to the same size as the pipe, and sealed with silicon sealant. The advantage of the coupler is that the pipework can be dismantled at any time without breaking the watertight seal. Connect enough flexible pipe to the coupler to reach the outlet of the pump and secure with a hose clip.

6 Connect a 10mm ($\frac{1}{2}$in) rigid copper pipe to the coupler on the inside of the urn. Cut the length of copper pipe so that the top is just below the rim of the urn.

7 Pass the loose end of the pipe through the brick pier and connect it to the outlet of the pump. Fill the urn and reservoir with water and check the fountain spout.

8 Place a permeable membrane, such as underlay, over the grid. Cover with cobbles and stones.

MAKING A COBBLE FOUNTAIN

YOU WILL NEED

- Plastic dustbin (trash can)
- Spade
- Soft sand
- Spirit level
- Hand trowel
- Timber for tamping the backfill
- Rake
- Cloth
- 2 bricks or a piece of broken paving
- Submersible pump
- Rigid delivery pipe with flow adjuster
- Tape measure
- Sheet of polythene (polyethylene)
- Scissors
- Galvanized metal mesh in two grades, both larger than the diameter of the dustbin
- Wire cutters
- Cobbles

This is one of the most popular of moving water features for small gardens because it is safe, easy to maintain and will fit into any size or style of garden.

A cobblestone fountain consists simply of water falling through a spout onto cobbles arranged around it, bringing movement and a gentle or turbulent sound. Such a feature is ideal for a patio, where it can be seen from indoors, and it also makes an ideal subject for garden lighting. An amber lens on a small low-voltage spotlight hidden by a nearby rock, for example, makes the water spout resemble the flames of a fire, providing an excuse for endless daydreaming.

The water level in the reservoir should be checked regularly if the fountain is used in hot, sunny weather. Water will evaporate from the cobbles in wind and sun, and if the pump is allowed to run dry the motor will be badly damaged. As a precaution, when using the fountain intermittently, pour 2 gallons of water into the reservoir before you turn it on.

1 Choose a small, level site near a window in an area of paving or in front of a border so that the fountain will provide a good focal point. The cobbles can be arranged in any shape or extend as far as you wish, but the area for the fountain need be no more than a circle with the diameter of a plastic dustbin (trash can). Mark out the diameter of the bin and dig out a hole slightly wider and deeper than its dimensions. Place a shallow layer of sand at the bottom of the hole.

2 Put the dustbin (trash can) in the hole to ensure that the rim is just level with the surrounding soil. Check that the sides are level by placing a spirit level across the top of the dustbin. If any corrections are necessary, lift out the bin and make adjustments to the bottom of the hole.

3 Backfill the gap between the bin and the sides of the hole with soil and ram firm with a piece of timber. Mound the surrounding soil slightly to make an even saucer shape and rake to remove any stones. Remove any soil that may have fallen into the bin, and wipe out the inside with a cloth.

4 Place two bricks at the bottom of the dustbin (trash can) to act as a plinth for the pump. This prevents the intake of any debris that accumulates at the base of the bin.

5 Check that the length of rigid plastic pipe used for the fountain spout from the pump will be 5–8cm (2–3in) higher than the sides of the dustbin (trash can).

6 Place the polythene (polyethylene) sheet over the bin (can) and surrounding area and cut out a hole slightly wider than the fountain pipe. Fill the bin with water.

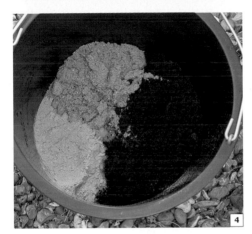

1 Stand the sink on a plinth that is smaller in width and length than the sink so that the coating does not stick to the support.

2 Hammer a cylindrical piece of wood into the outlet pipe at the bottom of the sink in order to retain the water.

3 Secure the bung by inserting a screw through the outlet pipe with a screwdriver. Seal around the bung with a silicon sealant.

4 Pour equal parts of sphagnum peat or peat substitute, sand or grit and cement into a plastic bucket in order to make the hypertufa.

5 Mix the hypertufa into a stiff mixture by slowly adding water and stirring.

6 Score the glazed exterior surface, including the rim, with a tile- or glass-cutter. Coat the sides and the rim of the sink with an industrial glue and allow it to become tacky.

7 Wearing rubber gloves and working from the bottom up, apply the stiff mixture of hypertufa to the sides and rim. The covering should be just thick enough to give a rough texture; if it is too thick it will not adhere. Protect the trough from rain and strong sunshine until the hypertufa is thoroughly dry; this could take as long as a week.

8 Coat the outside walls and rim with proprietary liquid fertilizer to encourage algae and moss to develop on the surface. Alternatively, you can paint the trough with antiquing fluid to create an aged effect. Paint the inside of the trough with black bitumen paint and allow to dry. Carefully move the trough to its permanent position and partly fill with water before planting with aquatics in small containers. A small amount of duckweed or other floater can be planted on the surface to reduce light and consequent water greening; this should be removed later, when the other plants become established.

For many water gardeners, a selection
of ornamental fish is the main reason
for having water. Fish provide great

FISH AND OTHER FAUNA

interest with their graceful movement
and colour, while at the same time
keeping pests and midge larvae from
building up. For a wildlife pool, fish
should not be considered a priority as
they eat many of the invertebrates
that make up a wildlife community.

OPPOSITE: **A stream is alive with
insects, birds and submerged life,
making complete the pleasure of
a wildlife-friendly feature.**

A BALANCED ECOSYSTEM

Examine a drop of pool water under a microscope and you will be amazed at the life on display. These tiny organisms are the basis of a clear, healthy and balanced pool. A diverse mix of organisms in the right proportions helps to prevent the growth of algae and provides the basis of a food chain that supports larger animals that bring so much added interest and pleasure.

THE FOOD CHAIN

Pond water hides a never-ending struggle for life. Fungi, worms, bacteria, nematodes and snails feed on organic debris, while further up the food chain, and preying on these tiny organisms, are the larvae of dragonflies, water beetles and crayfish. These are, in turn, eaten by fish, frogs, newts and salamanders. This intriguing web of life has a final layer of predation in the form of herons, kingfishers and, in tropical waters, alligators. The chain of feeding depends on size; for example, small fish fry are eaten by beetles, which die and become food for the worms. Maintaining the cycle in a natural wetland habitat should be the main goal in the sensitive management of an informal garden pool. Many gardeners will happily leave nature to develop a balance, but a man-made pool has not evolved naturally and so is prone to periodic upsets, particularly if the volume of water is very small.

BELOW: **The depth of the main part of this pool is over 1m (3ft). This will prevent marginal plants from taking over the pond, and destroying its natural balance.**

GREEN WATER AND ALGAE

A dramatic symptom of an imbalance in the pool's micro-organisms is green water, which is caused by excess algae. The algae are minute, single-celled organisms that thrive in sunlight, nutrient-rich water and warmth. Although they are a source of food to some members of the food chain, they are unlikely to be eaten in sufficient quantity in a small pool, and without competition they become dominant. They usually make their presence felt in a newly installed pool where there is an abundance of mineral salts and no competition from plants for the available nutrients. As soon as plants develop, they compete with the algae for food, and the shade from their leaves denies the algae the sunlight that is essential for their growth. The regular introduction of tapwater, which is rich in the chemicals on which the algae feed, also upsets this balance, and wherever possible rainwater should be used for any topping up.

The other type of algae that can become a nightmare to water gardeners is known as blanketweed, a filamentous algae that, unlike the free-floating, single-celled algae, attach themselves to higher plants or other objects. Blanketweed – *Spirogyra*, to give it its botanical name – gathers together in great masses, which are clearly visible in the water because it resembles green cotton wool. In spring these masses rise to the surface, buoyed up by the bubbles of oxygen – and a useful reminder of the value of all green plants as oxygenators.

OTHER AQUATIC FAUNA

One of the fascinations of a pool is the way insects seem to be able to walk over the surface of the water. There is an invisible elastic skin, the meniscus, supporting small creatures above and below it. A group of insects, including the pond skater and whirligig beetle, feed on the dead and dying insects that fall onto the surface of the water, but they are the least well adapted to aquatic life as they seldom need to go under the water. The larvae and pupae of gnats and mosquitoes, on the other hand, can suspend themselves under the film when they surface to take in air.

Away from the surface of clear water, aquatic leaves are a home to larvae, caterpillars and snails, which can become pests of ornamental plants by eating holes in

A CROSS-SECTION OF POND LIFE

Some of the more common inhabitants of the garden pool which
go towards forming a balanced ecosystem.

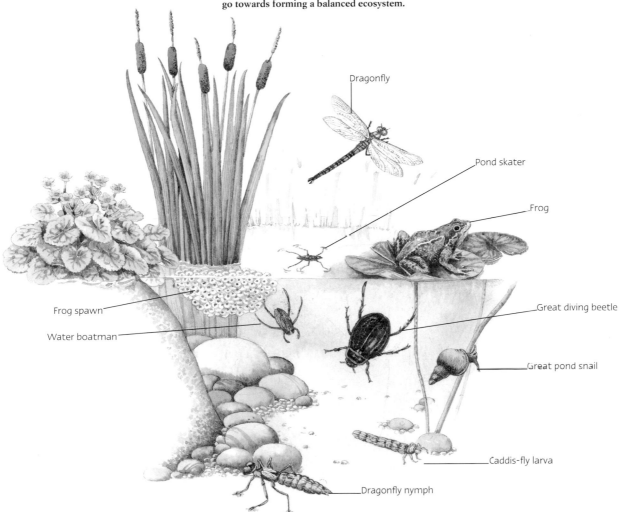

Dragonfly

Pond skater

Frog

Frog spawn

Water boatman

Great diving beetle

Great pond snail

Caddis-fly larva

Dragonfly nymph

the leaves. Preying on all of these are several carnivorous animals, such as the great diving beetle, the water boatman, the water scorpion and nymphs of dragonflies and damselflies. In the mud at the pool bottom are a number of specialized creatures that can survive in the deoxygenated conditions. The most common of these are the red bloodworm larvae of midges and, in larger pools, mussels, which dig their fleshy feet into the mud, taking in large quantities of water through a siphon tube, extracting oxygen and plankton and passing out the spent water through another tube.

The array of visitors to the pool, in the form of birds, grass snakes, frogs and water voles, is one of the reasons that gardeners develop an informal water garden to encourage wildlife. However, we must return to the open water, where, in contrast to the microscopic life, are the largest of the permanent pool dwellers, the fish.

LEFT: **Lush ferns by
the side of this shady
stream provide good
cover for birds,
snakes, amphibians
and mammals.**

STOCKING THE POOL

As we have seen, the biological balance of a pool is susceptible to upset in a small, artificial pool. The addition of large fish in too great a number can also upset this balance. In natural pools, the fish will have developed in the community, and their feeding habits will be in tune with the foodstuffs around them. Such fish are often bottom dwellers, not highly coloured, and in small pools or shallow streams they are generally small.

BELOW: **The colour and movement of fish bring life to this well-designed pool.**

HOW MANY FISH?

The impact on the pool of several large fish is far reaching. Apart from the physical disturbance to the soil around the roots in container plants, their mouthparts will be large enough to devour many of the lower forms of pool life that have hitherto contributed to the balance of the food chain. Fish should not, therefore, be added to a pool on impulse. Rather, the choice of species, their size, and the number that the pool will sustain in a healthy environment must be carefully considered. The maximum number that a pool will sustain is based on the surface area of the pool that is free from vegetation and the size of the fish. Volume of water is not used as a criterion in stocking because a very deep pool with only a small surface area does not absorb atmospheric oxygen as well as a shallow pool with a large surface area. Depth is, of course, important

LEFT: **The markings and colours of koi are very important to keen koi collectors.**

in providing protection in the winter and a stable temperature in the summer, but it is a secondary factor in determining stocking levels.

A good guideline to use in a still pool is not to exceed 5cm of body length of fish to 900 square centimetres (2in to 1 square foot) of surface area. Taken literally, this could become a choice of two or three very large fish or several smaller ones, but it is strongly recommended that you go for the latter option, that is, several smaller fish. You should also bear in mind that little fish will grow and that the calculation made when the fish were small may be inaccurate in two or three years' time.

The guideline is also based on the dimensions of a still pool. As soon as you introduce a watercourse or have a fountain playing constantly in summer, the oxygen levels are increased and the pool will support slightly larger numbers. If biological filtration is introduced as well, the number of fish can be increased even more.

The type of fish is also a factor in stocking levels, not only because of their ultimate size but also because of their habits, which make volume as well as surface area significant. Koi, for instance, have different requirements from goldfish, and, given their ultimate size,

they need a volume of water greater than 10,000 litres (2642 gallons) and a minimum area of 20 square metres (215 square feet). Again, if a filtration system is used, these figures can be reduced and if the fish are only small and removed to another pool when they get very large, the ultimate volume and size are not as important.

BELOW: **These goldfish and koi, which are on sale in an aquatic centre, are clamouring for food from all and sundry.**

TYPES OF FISH

There is a wide range of fish available to the gardener, but before buying it is important to consider not only the ultimate size of the fish in relation to the size of the pool, but also the type of fish in relation to the type of water feature you have. Koi, for example, will not only look out of place in a natural pool, but they might also have a deleterious effect on the food chain in such a pool. In a natural pool, where the aim is to provide a habitat for a wide range of plants and wildlife, less glamorous species will be a much more appropriate choice. In a smaller, formal pool, however, decorative and eye-catching goldfish can be introduced to enhance the overall appearance of the pool, and in such a pool the balance of plant life and animal life can be more easily controlled to accommodate the fish, making it more appropriate for exotic introductions.

BELOW: **The mixed colourings and patterns of these fish form an interesting mosaic against the dark water.**

GOLDFISH

The suitability of goldfish for ornamental pools was recognized centuries ago in China, where they were kept as pets during the Sung dynasty, which reigned from 960 to 1279. Breeding really got under way in Japan at the beginning of the 18th century, and since then several variants of the common goldfish have become available. With the more recent introduction of koi, however, the goldfish has become much undervalued, but it is one of the most adaptable of all pool fish, capable of living in total harmony with other species of fish and not causing upset to the plant life.

Goldfish can live for about 20 years and achieve a maximum length of 35cm (14in), weighing up to just over a kilogram (2¼lb). They are omnivorous, and they can tolerate high levels of acidity or alkalinity in

the water and much lower oxygen levels than most other ornamental fish. In addition, they can tolerate a wider range of temperature levels, although the optimum temperature is 22–25°C (72–77°F). Goldfish will breed easily, maturing when they are three or four years old. They prefer still, fairly shallow water, which is heavily planted. When they are very young they are almost transparent, turning brown and then the more familiar orange colour when they are about six months old.

COMET GOLDFISH

An attractive variant on the standard goldfish is the comet goldfish, which has a long body, growing to 38cm (15in), and extensive, graceful fins and tail. The comet has resulted from painstaking selections by breeders in the United States. Similar in shape to goldfish, these fish are extremely tolerant of a wide range of temperatures and can even survive in temperatures as low as 0°C (32°F). They feed at all levels in the water but need more space than the common goldfish. They are available in a variety of markings, from white to black and from gold to vermilion. Feeding with a high-protein flake brings out the red colouring.

SHUBUNKIN

The other hardy goldfish variant is the shubunkin, which is similar to the comet and available in a range of colours. The popular varieties feature mottling of black, red, purple, blue and brown under pearly scales. Extensively bred in Japan since the early years of the 20th century, the blue colorations are highly prized. They feed at all levels and will grow to 38cm (15in).

ORANDA AND BLACK MOORS

The oranda is similar to the fantail but has a more compact body, a longer tail and fins and an intriguing cap-like addition to the head. This is a delicate fish and should not be kept outdoors in winter in temperate climates.

The black moor, a black fantail, either fascinates or repels, with its extended goggle-like eyes. It is an egg-shaped fish, with a velvety-black body and long fins and tail. Black moors grow to about 12cm (4½in) long, and they feed at all levels. They should be kept indoors in winter. They belong to a large group of exotic varieties, including lionheads, celestials and red telescopes, which are mainly the province of the specialist fish-keeper in warm climates. Even in

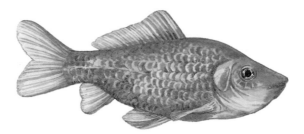

Common goldfish

Comet goldfish

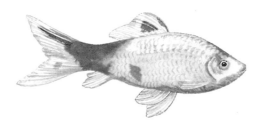

Shubunkin

Oranda

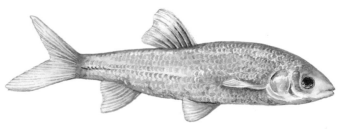

Golden orfe

Fantail

Koi

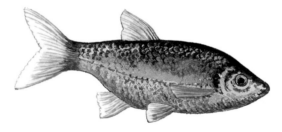

Golden rudd

Grass carp

Minnow

Stickleback

the summer months in a temperate climate, their appendages and bulky, flowing fins make them vulnerable to predators.

GOLDEN ORFE

The golden orfe are a favourite hardy fish for pools. When viewed from above, their sleek bodies are not unlike those of a trout, and they dart quickly around the pool in shoals. For this reason, it is important that you should introduce at least four of this species if this is your choice. They do, however, need space to move quickly so they are not the most suitable fish for a very small pool. They are a surface-swimming fish, which require plenty of oxygen, and they are among the first to suffer on warm nights in summer when oxygen levels are low.

Golden orfe are golden-yellow on top with silver-white undersides. They grow to 30–50cm (12–20in) in length and live for about 15 years. They are very effective at keeping down mosquito larvae, often leaping out of the water at high speed.

FANTAIL AND CALICO FANTAIL

Less hardy but beautiful fish for warmer climates are the fantails and the calico fantails. They have rather egg-shaped bodies and seldom exceed 9cm (3½in) in length. They have long, double tails. Extremely sedate swimmers, the fantail and calico fantail can be identified by their colouring. The fantail is a golden-orange with black-and-white splashes; the calico is a multicoloured form with patches of black, blue, red, white and gold. If the water temperature falls below 15°C (59°F) these fish should be moved indoors.

KOI

A visit to the fish department of an aquatic centre will quickly reveal what has become the most popular fish in recent years. This position in the popularity stakes must go to koi, which is the Japanese word for carp. As collectors' fish, they have a bewildering classification system related to their markings, and the fancy koi are strictly known as Nishikigoi or brocaded koi. Most enthusiasts are happy to refer to them as koi, however.

This is a fish that needs a special pool if you are going to become an enthusiast for the species, rather than an enthusiast for the water garden, because the two are not always compatible. Regrettably, people's appetites are whetted by the enormous specimens they see on display at aquatic centres, where the fish have highly coloured patterns and may even take food from the visitor's hand.

Small koi might seem an appealing buy for the pool, but you should remember that these fish can grow very large and a small pool will quickly become unsuitable for them. Being carp, they are bottom-feeders and their huge mouths blow and suck around the plant roots and oxygenators, causing the water to become cloudy and the plants to be dislodged. Ideally, koi should be kept in a pool that is specially designed to meet their particular requirements – they need high, vertical side walls, a bottom drain and a filtration system in their pool.

GOLDEN RUDD

If you have an informal or wildlife pool, you might want to consider keeping golden rudd, which are ideal candidates for the conditions in this type of pool. Similar in shape to the orfe but slightly fatter, these fish are covered with rather large and coarse silvery scales. They can reach 25cm (10in) in length and can be recognized by the reddish colour of the fins. Surface-feeders and tolerant of a wide range of temperatures, golden rudd will happily breed in a pool provided there is ample vegetation.

GRASS CARP

These fish, which are mostly imported from China, have become more widely available in recent years. They have voracious appetites for soft green vegetation, such as duckweed, and, if food is short, even for blanketweed, and they should, therefore, be introduced only if soft vegetation needs to be kept under control. They are silver-grey in colour, and their wide mouths are adapted to feeding on plants. They will grow quickly to 60cm (2ft) in length, so they need a large pool. They are middle- to bottom-feeders and will thrive in temperatures of 0–20°C (32–68°F).

MINNOWS AND STICKLEBACKS

In contrast to the grass carp, these fish do not require much space, and they are ideal for small wildlife pools. Minnows grow to 8–15cm (3–6in) and prefer clear, shallow, well-oxygenated water. Male fish develop a red coloration in the mating season. Sticklebacks are about the same size and, like minnows, prefer shallow water. Do not introduce more than two couples into a small pool because they become territorial and protective of their young.

LEFT: **The patternings and markings on fish is one of the reasons that they are so popular among pool owners.**

BELOW: **Feeding fish is one of the pleasures of keeping them. These koi are waiting in keen anticipation.**

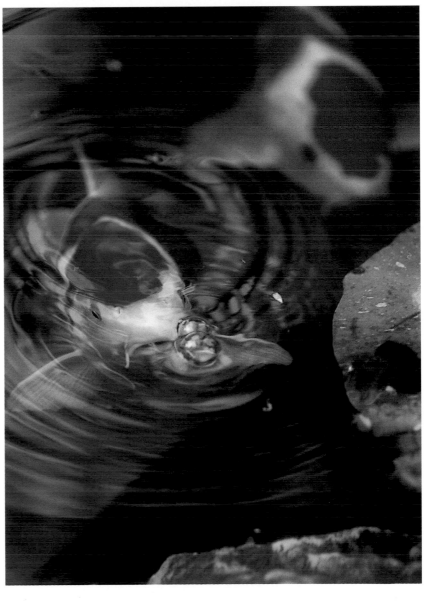

BUYING FISH

Because so many ornamental fish are imported, they can be very weak after transportation and a period in quarantine. It is sensible to search for a reliable supplier, who will have sorted out weak and damaged fish before placing his stock in display tanks for sale. A supplier who provides hygienic conditions for fish at this stage can do much to help reduce the incidence of diseases.

CHOOSING A HEALTHY FISH

The best time to buy fish is in late spring and summer, when the water temperature will be above 10°C (50°F). Try to buy in groups of six, as several fish seem to be less nervous than a single fish. Before buying, examine the fish carefully for damaged or missing scales because exposed tissue is vulnerable to infection. The larger the fish, the more likely it is that some scales will be missing because bigger fish are more aggressive in display tanks, and can damage themselves more easily.

Choose a fish that is lively. The dorsal fin should be erect, and the eyes bright. If the body shape seems slightly bent, this could be a sign of damage to the nervous system. Reject any fish that appears to be scraping itself against the bottom of the tank; this is an indication of a scale disorder. The more highly coloured the fish, the more likely it is that it has been only recently imported. If the tanks are under cover the colours will be more subdued, but the fish will be becoming more acclimatized to the quarantine conditions and therefore less vulnerable to infection.

Resist the urge to select large fish; instead, choose smaller ones, ideally 8–13cm (3–5in) long. At this size, they are not only cheaper, but will become acclimatized to new conditions more easily than larger fish.

A good supplier will place the fish in a small amount of water in a strong polythene (polyethylene) bag. Before sealing, pure oxygen will be pumped into the bag, and as long as the bag is not opened this will provide oxygen for at least 24 hours, depending on the number of fish. In warm weather get the fish home as quickly as possible because the temperature in the bag will rise very quickly. Place the bag inside a cardboard box with a lid so that light can be excluded during the journey. Keep the boxes in the boot of the car, as sunlight streaming through the windows onto the box will heat up the water. Do not lift the bag out of the box to examine the fish: this will cause unnecessary distress to the fish and possibly damage the fins.

Avoid introducing the fish to the pool immediately because the drop in temperature in the large volume of water in the pool would be a terrible shock to the fish. Instead, gently place the sealed bag on the surface of the pool and allow it to float there for a while so that the temperature inside the bag gradually matches the pool temperature. This will take about two hours.

Only then should you think about releasing the fish. Cut the neck of the bag and let in some of the pool water, then carefully let the fish escape. They will swim to the bottom, and if there is any cover in the pool they will hide. In a day or two the fish will become more inquisitive and a small amount of food can be given.

BELOW: **If handling is necessary, try to balance and secure the fish between the head and body with both hands.**

BELOW RIGHT: **After the journey from the supplier, immerse the bag in the pool for two hours to allow the temperature of the water to reach the same level as the pool before freeing the fish.**

FEEDING FISH

In a large, well-established pool that is amply stocked with plants and in which the number of fish does not exceed the recommended stocking rate by too much, there should be little need to give any supplementary feed. In smaller pools, however, it is important for you to provide extra food, and, to minimize pollution, the food should be carefully chosen and given in limited amounts.

WHEN TO FEED

The most important times to provide a food supplement are spring and autumn. Spring feeding boosts the fish after the winter period when they do not eat, and an autumn feed helps to build them up for winter. The water temperature plays an important part in a fish's need for food. If the water temperature is below 8°C (46°F), there is no need to feed; at this temperature the fish go into a semi-lethargic state and consume nothing. There are often mild intervals in the winter when the water temperature hovers around and sometimes exceeds this level and the fish become active. Resist the temptation to feed them as the food will remain undigested in the gut as soon as the temperature drops again.

As the temperature warms up in spring, begin feeding once a day at the same time and in the same place. Commercial preparations of suitable food have improved dramatically, particularly floating types that let you see if the food is being eaten. A high-protein food, such as floating pellets or flakes, is ideal. Give no more food than the fish can consume within five minutes. Overfeeding is not only wasteful, it will have a detrimental effect on the water chemistry, as the decomposing uneaten food will accumulate and pollute the water. Feeding little and often is generally a better approach as summer advances, and occasional treats, such as live water fleas (*Daphnia*), will be useful if the fish are breeding. Live food is often difficult to obtain, however, and supplements such as frozen shredded shrimp, dried flies and ants' eggs are often more easily obtained. Even food that is marketed principally for koi is suitable for other species if they are large enough. As the weather cools down again in autumn, gradually reduce the amount of food and use a wheatgerm pellet or flake in the cooler water.

If you have a small pool, missing feeding for a day or two will not be a problem, but arrange for a friend to feed the fish if you are to be away for a week or two.

FISH PROBLEMS

Dragonfly

Dragonfly larva
attacking a fish

Damselfly

Damselfly
larva

Great diving beetle

The majority of fish will survive and flourish happily for many years. Provided you have chosen the right type of fish and your pool is not overstocked, the fish should survive and even, in time, breed. From time to time, however, even in a well-balanced and well-maintained pool, the fish may suffer from a variety of problems, including diseases and pests.

FISH DISEASES AND OTHER PROBLEMS

Diseases are often introduced into a pool with a new fish, and this is why it is important to obtain your fish from a good supplier. Fish that are under stress because of poor environmental conditions – such as insufficient volume of water, pollution, overcrowding, lack of oxygen and insufficient or poor food – are susceptible to infection.

No matter how careful you are, however, it is almost inevitable that your fish will, at some point, be affected by disease, and the following disorders are the most common. Where practicable, home treatments are indicated. If you are in any doubt, seek the advice of the vet and do not make matters worse by incorrect handling. If you use a proprietary treatment, make sure that it is diluted with clean water as indicated by the manufacturer.

Dropsy This bacterial disease causes swollen bellies, lethargy, bristling scales and sunken or staring eyes. If the attack is very acute the fish will die rapidly, but it is often sick for several weeks before it dies. The bacteria are present in all expanses of water, and a healthy fish will produce enough antibodies to fight infection. Consult a fish specialist if you suspect this disease.

Bacteria can also be responsible for ulcers, which are easier to identify and can only be treated if they are caught very early on.

Fungal infections The most common fungus is referred to as "cotton wool fungus" or "cotton wool disease". Fungi grow on the damaged skin of weak fish and, if left untreated, the fungus is invaded by toxins and the fish dies. There is also a disease known as fin rot or tail rot, which attacks more decorative types of goldfish with long fins. The diseased area becomes ragged or bloodshot.

Both these ailments can be treated by a proprietary treatment, administered by placing the fish into a separate tank. Sea salt is sometimes recommended as an

effective remedy. Small quantities of sea salt are added to the water to a level of 10g per litre (¼oz per 2 pints). When the fungus is cured, start to replace the saltwater with fresh water. Working at two-hourly intervals and using fresh water at room temperature, change one-third of the water, then one-half and then another half.

Loss of balance Occasionally a fish may be swimming on its side or suspended upside-down. Constipation through eating too much dried food of the wrong type may be the cause, but more often it is a problem of the swim bladder, the fish's balancing mechanism. The kindest answer is to kill the fish by a sharp tap on the head.

Parasites Fish seen rubbing themselves on the bottom of the pool is a sign of parasitic infection. In severe cases, the fish may secrete a grey mucus, become listless and clamp its fins close to its body. Treat individually with a proprietary treatment in a quarantine tank.

White spot The early stages of fungus infection should not be confused with this disease, which is caused by a tiny parasite. Be careful, too, not to confuse the spots with white pimples that occur on the gill plates of male fish during the mating season. The symptoms of white spot are tiny, clearly defined white spots on the body and fins. In order to ease the irritation that the spots cause, the infected fish will be seen scraping themselves on the bottom or sides of the pool. Treatment tends to be effective only if the infection is caught early. Try the proprietary treatments that can be added to the pool as a whole before resorting to one of the specialist treatments for individual fish in isolation.

A DISEASED FISH

Fish can succumb to a number of unpleasant diseases, some of which are shown here.

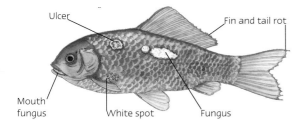

Ulcer — Fin and tail rot — Mouth fungus — White spot — Fungus

FISH PESTS

Ornamental fish are prone to attack from pests and predators from both outside and within the pool. Dense planting of strong species will deter most cats, and an overlapping paved edge will provide a hiding place for fish. More serious are birds like kingfishers and herons.

Herons The heron is a fish's most serious enemy, even in relatively built-up areas, and control against them is difficult. A standard recommendation is to surround the pool with two inconspicuous horizontal wires, one at a height of about 45cm (18in) and the other 75–90cm (30–36in), held on closely spaced canes to keep the wires taut. As the heron walks towards the pool, it should be alarmed as it reaches the water and fly off. There is a range of proprietary guards on the market, the best of which relies on a similar line held under tension. When it is touched, it releases a catch that explodes a cap to startle the bird. Decoy herons are often tried, but their guile tends to overcome all but the most skilful of defences.

Great diving beetle This is a real menace to fish fry and small species of fish. The adult beetle has a dark brown body with a distinctive gold or yellow edge and

reaches a length of 5cm (2in). It lives for nearly three years, mostly in the water. It flies only at night and survives underwater by storing oxygen in its wing cases. It preys on newts, tadpoles and small fish and is difficult to eradicate. Try to catch it in a net immediately.

Dragonfly and damselfly larvae These larvae have a scorpion-like outline and a "mask", which shoots out to catch passing fish. The green to brown nymphs can live for up to five years on the pool bottom, during which time they devour a large number of small fish with the lobster-like claws on the "mask", which they use to pull the victim into the mouthparts. The only method of control is to remove the larvae by hand, a job so unpleasant that it is seldom practised.

Water boatmen Few people realize that this insect can be an aggressive predator of small fish. Although only 10–15mm (about ½in) long, it can kill a small fish by injecting poison through its piercing mouthparts. Netting is the only effective method of control.

Whirligig beetle Another frequently seen inhabitant of the summer pool is the whirligig beetle, which can be seen in groups of 20 or more at a time. The black, oval beetles are only 3–5mm (⅛–¼in) long, and although they are air-breathing insects, they spend nearly half their lives in water. They do this by creating an air bubble to breathe as they dive for food on the pool bottom. They are too small to inflict damage on adult fish, but are a pest for fish fry. To control, net off from the surface of the water.

Water scorpion This pest lives in shallow water from which they seldom move. They are about 2.5cm (1in) long, and, being poor swimmers they remain motionless. The snorkel-like spine at the tip of the body enables them to breathe from the surface. It will grab small fish with its pincer-like legs, while the sharp mouthparts pierce the fish and kill it. Apart from removal by hand, hygiene in the small pool is the only method of control.

Leeches, lice and anchor worms These predatory creatures attach themselves to the side fins or gills. They are large enough to see with the naked eye and can be removed with tweezers. Proprietary antiseptics should always be used to disinfect small wounds after removal. There are other chemical treatments if you find yourself unable to perform these surgical tasks with tweezers.

Water boatman

Water scorpion

Whirligig beetle

Clockwise from left: Anchor worm, leech and louse

Heron

OPPOSITE: **Cotton wool fungus on the tail of a minnow.**

LEFT: **Cotton or fishing line above the water deters herons.**

An ample supply of water leads to extensive plant growth both under the water and in the shallow margins.

CARE AND MAINTENANCE

This growth dies down in winter in temperate climates and leads to a build up of rotting vegetation. Regular maintenance is thus vital in a well-stocked pool to keep a healthy balance and to prevent it becoming a reservoir of pea-green water.

OPPOSITE: Autumn leaves on the surface of a pond create fleeting compositions, but should not be allowed to build up.

STRUCTURAL REPAIRS

In summer evaporation will probably cause a drop in the level of the water in the pool of about 1cm (½in) a week, and in very hot weather the water loss may be even greater. There are, however, other reasons for a drop in the water level, and if your pool seems to be losing water all year round, it might be because it is damaged. The main problem with a leak is locating it. Normally, the water level will remain just below the damage, so this line becomes the starting point for detailed examination.

REPAIRING A CONCRETE POOL

Concrete pools develop hair-line cracks over the years, as the earth surrounding the pool moves slightly. A crack may extend in any direction, so it is advisable to drain the water away well below the suspect area so that the surface of the concrete can dry out thoroughly. Clean the damaged area with a wire brush or scrubbing bush and wash it thoroughly. When the surface has dried again use a thin stone chisel in order to widen and deepen the crack slightly, by tapping gently along the length of the crack. Thoroughly brush out the enlarged crack and the immediate surrounding area with a wire brush. Then fill the crack with new mortar, using a small flat-pointed trowel. Allow the mortar to dry for 48 hours and then apply a proprietary sealant.

With old concrete pools this is only likely to be a temporary improvement, and a fresh crack may occur quite soon afterwards. It is often more sensible to line the whole concrete pool with a flexible liner, which is both a long lasting and an effective remedy and is likely to be far less costly than it may first appear, particularly when the time and trouble involved in repairing the concrete are taken into account.

REPAIRING PREFORMED POOLS

A preformed unit can succumb to irregular ground pressure around the pool by developing cracks. Fibreglass units can be repaired by using the repair kits that are sold for patching holes or cracks in motor vehicles and that contain a piece of matting, which has a mesh structure to bond the repair better. Roughen the damaged area with sandpaper and clean it thoroughly. Then apply the fibreglass matting repair to cover an area that is greater in all directions than the damaged area. Follow the instructions given with the repair kit and allow a minimum of 24 hours for the compound to dry.

REPAIRING FLEXIBLE LINERS

Modern, high-quality, flexible liners are far less prone to leaks than old concrete pools and the old-style flexible liners. Suppliers of liners also sell repair kits that make the job of patching a flexible liner quite straightforward. Black double-sided adhesive waterproof tape will be adequate for small punctures or tears in the liner. The damaged area must be thoroughly

FIXING A CONCRETE POOL

Hair-line cracks in concrete pools can be repaired by filling with new mortar.

1 Clean the damaged area with a wire brush and wash thoroughly. Use a stone chisel to enlarge the crack.

2 Brush out the enlarged crack thoroughly with the wire brush and fill in with fresh mortar, using a small, flat-pointed trowel.

3 Allow the fresh mortar to dry for 48 hours and then apply a proprietary sealant.

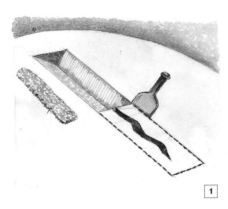

cleaned and dried: wipe it with a soft cloth dampened with spirit. Apply the tape over the hole and remove the protective cover on the tape, allowing the surface to become tacky. A patch from a spare piece of liner should then be pressed on to the tape. Make sure that the edges are well firmed. Wait at least 12 hours before refilling the pool.

If there is a watercourse or waterfall the leak may not be in the reservoir main pool but in the stream system itself. Check this by turning off the pump when the bottom pool is quite full and wait a day to see if there is any drop in the level. If the water level remains constant the leak is likely to be in the watercourse, and each individual waterfall and stream section will have to be dried out and cleaned to identify the position of the leak.

REPAIRING CLAY-LINED POOLS

Penetration by the roots of trees is the most common reason for a leak in a clay-lined pool. The shallower parts of the sides may also be suspect if the clay has been allowed to dry out in a prolonged hot spell when the water level might have dropped significantly.

The powdered form of bentonite comes into its own as a repair material for a clay lining. Finding the right place to apply it poses much the same problem as locating the leak in a flexible liner or concrete pool. Tracers such as vegetable dyes can be used to indicate the position of the leak, for there will be a higher concentration of the dye at the point of the leak if the pool is emptied. If soil covered the clay lining, it will have been eroded by the leak and could be a good clue to finding the place where the water has been leaking away. Once you have located the leak, apply an ample covering, about 8–10cm (3–4in), of bentonite powder over the suspect point and the area immediately surrounding it. Cover this with an additional 23–30cm (9–12in) of soil before reintroducing the water.

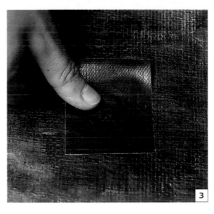

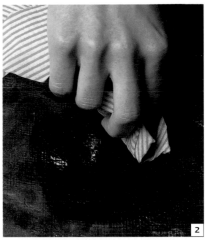

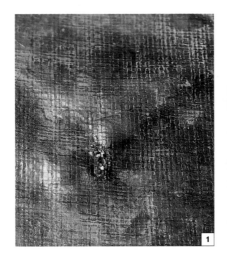

MENDING A FLEXIBLE LINER

Most modern liners are less prone to leaking than earlier makes. If a leak does occur, it is easy to repair.

1 Damage to liners, such as holes that have reached this size, will soon drain a small pond. Finer tears may need the liner lifting to the light to see the tear clearly.

2 Clean the damaged area very carefully with a cloth that has been dampened first with methylated spirits.

3 Use black, double-sided, adhesive waterproof tape to stick a small piece of liner over the tear.

FIXING A PREFORMED UNIT

Preformed units that are made from fibreglass can be easily repaired using a repair kit which is similar to that sold for patching holes or cracks in cars. The patch is made from a very thin, meshed material.

1 Clean the damaged area with a cloth that has been dampened with methylated spirits.

2 Using a large paintbrush, paint over the crack with adhesive.

3 Glue the patch over the crack and seal with a proprietary sealant.

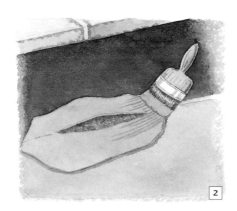

WATER QUALITY

The colour of the water is a very good indicator of its quality. The most common problem is green water, which is associated with an excess of tiny algae feeding on mineral salts. Do not use tap water when topping up the pool because this contains high levels of salts. Collect rainwater in a butt and use this for topping up.

Water that takes on other shades, however, may be suffering from some of the less common disorders. Brown water is most often caused by the constant disturbance of the pond bottom by fish which churn up the mud and cause myriads of fine particles to be held in suspension in the water. This can be remedied by the use of pond treatments called flocculators which cause all the tiny particles to clump together and sink

to the bottom. There is little point in doing this if the fish constantly disturb the mud, so a complete clean out to remove all the organic matter on the bottom will be necessary. Alternatively, the fish can be removed or the species of fish changed. Koi will churn up the bottom and if the fish are big, the problem gets worse. If bottom mud is likely to be a permanent feature, use surface swimming fish like orfe to reduce the problem.

Very dark water or black water is mainly a sign of excess rotting vegetation on the pond bottom. Where oxygenators have not been trimmed back enough or yellow and brown waterlily leaves have not been removed, they build up and decay on the bottom. Where this is excessive the water gradually becomes

BELOW: **Top up the level of the water in the pool in the summer when evaporation levels are high. This is very important if you have a watercourse running continuously.**

darker and blackens, and this is not possible to control by chemicals. If the matter cannot be removed, then partial water changes are the only alternative. This means changing no more than approximately one-third of the pool volume about every six weeks to reduce the concentration of brackish water in the pond.

Milky water is also a sign of some rotting organism on the bottom. The pond may be otherwise quite clean and the milkiness appears only in the summer when the water warms up. More often than not in a small pool this is caused by a dead animal, such as a frog, toad or even a rodent which may have fallen in.

Sometimes oily patches float about on the surface during the summer. This is caused by waterlily leaves dying and rotting on the surface. Remove any dying leaves as soon as they appear and then lay newspaper on the water surface to absorb the oil.

LEFT: **Algae and blanketweed can soon build up on the intake of pumps. Clean strainers and inlet holes regularly.**

BELOW: **At the first signs of autumn leaf fall, suspend a fine plastic net over the pond surface to prevent leaves sinking into the water.**

LEFT: **An overflow pipe connected from a rainwater butt to the pool is a useful way of reducing the need to use mains water when topping up.**

PLANT CONTROL

An aquatic environment is one of rapid and extensive growth, resulting in time in an overgrown pond surface if no control is practised. The main task in maintaining ponds is undoubtedly the constant cutting back of excess vegetation. In a small pond this is not too much of a burden, but in larger ponds where there is a natural bottom of mud, this is a time-consuming process. There are several submerged oxygenators like *Myriophyllum* (milfoil), which, if allowed to grow unchecked, would completely swamp a small pond in no time. Similarly there are marginals capable of forming rafts of floating roots into the deeper water, and over a number of years such ponds lose the water surface completely.

Fortunately the domestic ornamental pond makes use of aquatic containers to restrain growth, it normally has a lined bottom rather than mud, and there is the opportunity to choose the species in the pond rather than it becoming naturalized with rampant indigenous species.

Late spring can be a difficult time to keep down blanketweed as the waterlily leaves have not yet fully grown and cut down light. Consequently the clear water surface receives high intensity spring sunshine, and as the water warms up so the blanketweed capitalizes

on the conditions. Reduce as much of the growth as possible by hand using a split cane or a proprietary device with wire coils on the end of a long shank. Even if the blanketweed is to be treated chemically, it is best to remove as much as possible first as its rapid death can lead to a shortage of oxygen in the water when large masses decompose.

TOP RIGHT: **Numerous tiny creatures live in blanketweed, and the removed weed should be left at the side for a while until the creatures can escape and return to the water.**

RIGHT: **To clear water of blanketweed, insert a cane into the water and twist it to wind the weed around it, rather like candyfloss.**

As the summer progresses the submerged oxygenators, which enjoy the warmer water, try to reach the sunlight and can spread quickly across the water surface. As they have such poor root systems, they can be removed by tools such as wire rakes which catch the stems. In smaller ponds where this would be too severe they can be simply cut back with shears.

The free-floating plants on small ponds are much easier to remove and you will find that a large net will be adequate for the job. Floaters such as the water soldier (*Stratiotes*) are more of a problem in that they sink partially during part of their life cycle and are therefore more difficult to reach and net out in the deeper water.

ABOVE: **Oxygenators and floaters can soon take over small ponds. Keep removing excess growth with a net.**

ABOVE LEFT: **Duckweed or other floaters can be useful initially in preventing green water, but they soon spread and need constant thinning.**

LEFT: **When oxygenating plants become congested, lift out clumps and tear them apart, returning about a half to two-thirds to the water.**

FAR LEFT: **Remove duckweed before it has a chance to spread. You will need to check for it on a regular basis.**

CLEANING OUT THE POOL

RIGHT: Waterlily leaves thrusting in dense clusters above the water surface are a sure sign that the plant needs lifting and dividing.

Even if you follow a regular maintanance programme, the pool will need to be completely cleaned out every few years, depending on its style, size and site. There will, inevitably, be an accumulation of mulm on the pool bottom, submerged plants and waterlilies become overgrown, and marginals will benefit from being divided and given a new start. The process of cleaning out the pool will, however, mean that the balance of life achieved over the years is going to be severely disrupted, and everything should be done to renew the harmony that was achieved.

The timing of the operation is the first important decision. If it is tackled too early in the spring, there is a risk of harming overwintering amphibians or young hatching offspring that are not old enough to fend for themselves. If it is tackled too late in the autumn, plants and creatures may not have time to recover before winter. Cleaning out a pool in midwinter would cause a great deal of damage by disturbing hibernating creatures.

THE POOL CLEAN-OUT

A pool needs to be cleaned out every few years in addition to following your normal maintenance programme. The best time to carry out this task is mid- to late summer. The following points should serve as a helpful step-by-step sequence for completely overhauling your pond:

- Start pumping out the water, filling a temporary pool for any fish
- Begin to net any fish before there is too much disturbance to the pool
- Remove containers of marginals from the shelves. They will not need immersing in the temporary pool provided they are not out of the water for more than two or three days
- Net out the remaining fish as the water gets shallower and before the mud gets too disturbed on the bottom. Start the aerator in the temporary pool and place a net over the top

- Lift out the containers from the bottom of the pool. These can be extremely heavy and may need sliding out over the edge; take care that you do not damage the flexible liner when you are doing this. If you have waterlilies or other deep-water aquatics, cover the leaves with wet newspaper while they are left standing at the side of the pool. Remove healthy young growth of the oxygenators and submerge in containers at the side
- As soon as it is difficult for the pump to operate, bale out the remaining water and mud. Keep about half a bucket of mud to reintroduce a small amount of microscopic life into the clean pool
- Rinse and brush the sides. Check for any possible damage to the liner and, if necessary, reinforce with patches of repair tape

- Divide and repot the waterlilies, using fresh aquatic compost (soil mix)
- Begin to refill the pool as soon as possible in order to return the fish, waterlilies and freshly planted cuttings of the oxygenators back into the pool.
- Return the fish, some of the old mud and the old pool water from the temporary pool
- Divide and repot the marginals and replace them on the marginal shelves
- Do not fill the pool to the very top until the new leaves from the waterlilies reach the surface; alternatively, place some temporary bricks under the containers until the plants are growing again, when the bricks can be removed
- Scatter ample floating-leaved plants on the surface of the pool in order to create shade for a few weeks when the balance of the pool will be returning to normal

This leaves mid- to late summer as the time when least damage will be done, and it allows plants to become re-established before the onset of winter.

The main problem with carrying out the work in summer will be the temporary care of the fish during what might be a hot spell. Adequate measures for their temporary housing should be planned well in advance, and every effort must be made to maintain adequate oxygen levels, even if this means using a small aerating block in the short-term accommodation. Depending on the size and quantity of the fish, children's paddling pools make good temporary housing, and a net placed across the top will prevent a cat or heron from exploiting the vulnerable fish and the fish from leaping out in fear. If possible, choose an overcast day: this is a hot and smelly job, and there will be less stress to plants and fish if it is cool.

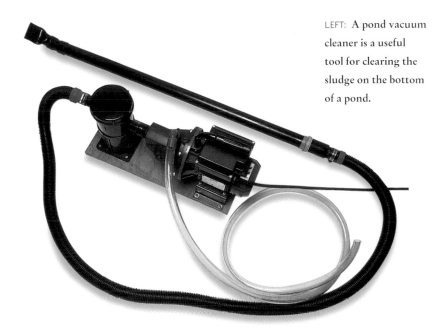

LEFT: **A pond vacuum cleaner is a useful tool for clearing the sludge on the bottom of a pond.**

PROTECTING POND PUMPS

If you leave a pump in your pond over winter, ice may damage it, so store it in a dry place, rather than simply take it out of the pond and leave it where moisture can enter.

1 Remove submersible pumps from the water before penetrating frosts cause the water to freeze deeply.

2 Clean the pump before you put it away. It will probably be covered with algae which can be scrubbed off.

3 Remove the filter and either replace it or clean it. Follow the instructions provided by the manufacturer.

4 Make sure all the water is drained from the pump. If your pump is an external one, make sure the system is drained.

5 Read the manufacturer's instructions, and carry out any other servicing that is necessary before storing the pump in a dry place. It may be necesssary to send it away for a service, in which case do it now instead of waiting until spring.

CALENDAR OF CARE

It would be misleading to suggest that introducing a pool into the garden is an easy option, but the ever-changing delights of the pool and its plants combined with the wildlife both within the water and attracted to it make any extra work more than worth it. Once your pool is built and the plants are established, the work needed to keep it looking its best soon becomes routine, and the main seasonal tasks are summarized here.

SPRING

• If an electric heater has been kept in the pool for the winter, it can be removed now and the filter started up if it was turned off for the winter.

• Any brown stems left on marginal and moisture-loving plants for winter attraction or protection for shy creatures can be cut back. Ornamental grasses should be pruned to just above the new green shoots.

• Plant any new moisture-loving plants or alpines.

• Herons are at their hungriest in spring, so take the necessary precautions to protect fish.

• Start feeding the fish again, offering small quantities of a high-protein food as soon as the water temperature climbs above 10°C (50°F). Check the fish for any disorders to which they may have succumbed in winter.

• Clean off algae from paved or wooden surfaces.

• Protect sensitive plants, such as skunk cabbage (*Lysichiton*), by placing horticultural fleece over the flowers if late frosts are forecast. The young growth of plants, such as giant rhubarb (*Gunnera manicata*), should have a protective covering of dead leaves until all danger of frosts has passed.

• Cut back the shoots of coppiced waterside shrubs, such as dogwoods (*Cornus*) and the coloured-stemmed willow (*Salix*).

• The young growth of tender marginals such as *Mimulus* and *Lobelia*, which has been protected by thick organic mulches, will be sprouting. Lift the plants and divide them or take cuttings of the young shoots and root them in a frost-free greenhouse.

• Strong spring sunshine could spark off algal growth in shallow pools where the surface is clear until the waterlily leaves begin to grow. This should correct itself as the surface leaves develop.

SUMMER

• Now is a good time to propagate any plants that have become overgrown or if extra plants are needed.

• Everything should be in full growth, particularly the oxygenators. Keep cutting these back so that the submerged shoots do not spread to the surface and become overgrown.

• Pests such as blackfly or thrips on waterlily leaves can be jetted off with a strong hose.

• Some sappy marginals, such as marsh marigolds (*Caltha palustris*), develop mildew in early summer.

BELOW: **In spring, prune shrubs, such as dogwood (*Cornus*), which grow by the side of the water.**

BELOW RIGHT:
Summer is a good time to propagate any plants that have become overgrown or if you need more plants for a pond.

Cut off affected leaves completely; they will soon grow again.

• Fish are very active now, but do not be tempted to overfeed. Feed little and often, and never with more than they can eat in five minutes.

• Slow-release pellets or sachets of fertilizer are sold for aquatics, particularly waterlilies. Push these just under the surface of the compost (soil mix).

• The meshes on submersible pumps will clog quickly if there is any blanketweed near the pump. Check regularly to keep this clear because it reduces the efficiency of the pump.

• If there are fish in the pool, keep the pump running for watercourses or fountains on hot nights to help maintain oxygen levels. If there is no pump, spray the surface of the water with a hosepipe.

• Remove blanketweed so that it does not develop into thick mats, which can entangle small fish.

• Tender floating plants, such as water hyacinth (*Eichhornia*) and water lettuce (*Pistia*), can be introduced to add interest.

AUTUMN

• Thin out and cut back the oxygenators because this growth will rot in the water over winter causing deoxygenation and pollution.

• If the weather continues to be warm, fish should be offered a high fibre food such as wheatgerm pellets until the water temperature drops to 10°C (50°F).

• Protect frost-tender marginals by providing a heavy, organic mulch over the crowns. As the first frosts blacken large-leaved plants such as *Rheum* and *Gunnera*, lay the plants' own blackened leaves and other dead leaves over the crowns of the plants to protect them for the winter.

• Net the surface of the pool to prevent autumn leaves from blowing into the water.

• Remove tender floating plants and store them indoors in a frost-free place on compost (soil mix) that is kept saturated.

WINTER

• If the winter is severe ice can be a problem if it covers the pool for prolonged periods. Methane gas, which is given off by decomposing vegetation, forms under the surface of the ice instead of being released to the atmosphere, and, because it is unable to escape, the methane is reabsorbed by the water, which becomes toxic to the fish. Use an electric

heater to keep a small circle of the pool's surface free of ice. Alternatively, place a hot pan on the ice until it melts a hole and repeat this daily until the ice thaws. Never break the ice by smashing through with a hammer, as this causes shock waves in the water that can damage the torpid fish.

• The expansion of thick ice can damage the sides of the pool. A pool with vertical side walls is more likely to be damaged than one with sloping sides. Placing objects such as spongy balls or pieces of wood in the water helps to absorb the pressure.

• If the pump is still operating a watercourse, lift it from the bottom so that it circulates colder water near the surface and does not disturb the beneficial layer of warmer water at the bottom of the pool.

• If spells of mild weather trigger activity by the fish do not be tempted to feed them.

• Brush snow off the ice to allow light into the pool.

• If there are long periods of drying winds that cause the level of the pool to drop it is as important to top up in these periods as it is in the summer.

• Net off any stray leaves that fall in the pool in gales.

• The dwarfer forms of waterlily may be damaged by severe cold in shallow pools. Remove them to a frost-free container full of water until the weather improves.

ABOVE: **Ice forming on the surface should not be allowed to persist for long periods without an air hole if fish are present.**

SUPPLIERS

United Kingdom

General distributors of a wide range of water garden products

Blagden Water Gardens
Bath Road
Upper Langford
North Somerset BS18 7DN
Tel: 01934 853531

Bradshaws
Nicolson Link
Clifton Moor
York YO1 1SS
Tel: 01904 691169

Heissner UK Ltd.
Regency Business Centre
Queens Road
Kenilworth
Warwickshire CV8 1JQ
Tel: 01926 851166
Fax: 01926 851151
email: heissner@regency
businesscentre.co.uk

Hozelock Cyprio Ltd.
Waterslade House
Haddenham
Aylesbury
Buckinghamshire HP17 8JD
Tel: 01844 291881

Lotus Water Garden Products
P.O. Box 36
Junction Street
Burnley
Lancashire BB12 ONA
Tel: 01282 420771

Oase (UK) Ltd.
3 Telford Gate
Whittle Road
West Portway Industrial Estate
Andover
Hampshire SP10 3SF
Tel: 01264 333225

Stapeley Water Gardens Ltd.
London Road
Stapeley
Nantwich
Cheshire
CW5 7LH
Tel: 01270 623868

Trident Water Garden Products
Carlton Road
Folehill
Coventry CV6 7FL
Tel: 024 7663 8802

Specialist Suppliers

Civil Engineering Developments Ltd.
728 London Road
West Thurrock
Grays
Essex RM16 1LU
Tel: 01708 867237
Rock supplier

Interpret
Interpret House
Vincent Lane
Dorking
Surrey RH4 3YX
Tel: 01306 881033
Fish foods and medicines

Pinks Hill Landscape Merchants
Broad Street
Wood Street Village
Guildford
Surrey
Tel: 01483 571620
Rock supplier

Rein Ltd.
Clifton Hall
Ashbourne
Derbyshire DE6 2GL
Tel: 01335 342265
Reinforced fibres for mortar

Tetra
Lambert Court
Chestnut Avenue
Eastleigh
Hampshire SO53 3ZQ
Tel: 023 8064 3339
Fish foods and medicines

Volclay Limited
Leonard House
Scotts Quay
Birkenhead
Merseyside L41 1FB
Tel: 0151 638 0967
Clay liners

Wychwood Waterlily and Carp Farm
Farnham Road
Odiham
Hook
Hampshire RG29 1HS
Tel: 0256 702800
Fish supplier

UNITED STATES

General distributors of a wide range of water garden products

Hyannis Country Garden
380 West Main Street
Hyannis, MA 02601
www.gardengoods.com

M&S Ponds and Supplies
14053 Midland Road
Poway, CA 92064
Tel: (858) 679-8729
Fax: (858) 679-5804

North American Rock Garden Society
P.O. Box 67
Millwood, NY 10546
www.hubris.net/nargs.org

Speciality Suppliers

Garden Rock Covers
P.O. Box 1133
Friday Harbor, WA98250
www.gardenrockcovers.com

Select Stone Inc.
P.O. Box 6403
Bozeman, MT 59771
Tel: (406) 582-1000
Fax: (406) 582-1069
www.selectstone.com

Sticks and Stones Farm
197 Huntingtown Road
Newtown, CT 06470
www.sticksandstonesfarm.com

CANADA

Aquascape Ontario
9295 Colborne Street Ext
Chatham
ON N7M 5J4
Tel: (888) 547-POND
Fax: (519) 352-1357

Aquatics & Co.
Box 445
Pickering, ON N7M 5J4
Tel: (905) 668-5326
Fax: (905) 668-4518
www.aquaticsco.com

Burns Water Gardens
RR2, 2419 Van Luven Road
Baltimore, ON KOK 1CO
Tel: (905) 372-2737
Fax: (905) 372-8625
www.eagle.ca/-wtrgdn

Picov's Water Garden Centre
and Fisheries
380 Kingston Road East
Ajax, ON L1S 4S7
Tel: (905) 686-2151
Fax: (905) 686-2183
www.picovs.com

Water Arts Inc.
4158 Dundas Street West
Etoklcoke, ON M8X 1X3
Tel: (416) 239-5345
Fax: (416) 237-1098

AUSTRALIA

Classic Garden Products
18 Baretta Road
Wangara, WA 6065
Tel: (61) 8 9409 6101

Diamond Valley Garden Centre
170 Yan Yea Road
Plenty Vic 3090
Tel: (61) 3 9432 5113

Ponds & Pumps
6 Parkview Drive
Archerfield Qld 4107
Tel: (61) 7 3276 7666

Universal Rocks
39 Stanley Street
Peakhurst NSW 2210
Tel: (61) 2 9533 7400

Waterproofing Technologies
Level 1, 210 Homer Street
Earlwood, NSW 2206
Tel: (61) 2 9558 2161
Pond liners

INDEX

ACKNOWLEDGEMENTS

KEY   l = left r = right t = top b = bottom c = centre

All the specially commissioned photographs in this book were taken by Peter Anderson with the exception of the following:
Jonathan Buckley: 17b; 19t; 45b (Chelsea 2000); 126 (Chelsea 2000).
Sarah Cuttle: 3c and 4 (designer: Simon Harman); 5l; 55; 62 (designer: Simon Harman); 68 (Hampton Court 2000); 80 (Longstock Water Gardens); 122br (Hampton Court 2000); 124; **Simon McBride**: 125.
Jo Whitworth: 54; 72r.

The publishers would like to thank the following for kindly allowing their images to be reproduced in this book:
Heather Angel: 110br. **A–Z Botanical Collection**: 6 (Adrian Thomas); 53tr (P. Etchells) **BBC Natural History Unit Picture Library**: **Jonathan Buckley**: 6 (Glen Chantry, Essex); **FLPA**: 103b (Linda Lewis). **Garden Exposures Picture Library**: photography copyright Andrea Jones 22 (Chelsea 2000). **The Garden Picture Library**: 8 (Ron Sutherland); 13t (Ron Sutherland); 15t (Ron Sutherland); 15b (Bob Challinor); 16 (Ron Sutherland); 17t (Gary Rogers); 19b (JS Sira); 20 (John Glover); 23t (Howard Rice); 24 (Tim Griffith); 25t (John Glover); 25c (Martine Mouchy); 38 (Mayer/Le Scanff); 40 (Marie O'Hara); 45t (Marie O'Hara); 46 (Bob Challinor); 47 (JS Sira); 50 (Christi

Carter); 66 (Ron Sutherland); 72tl (David Askham); 72b (John Glover); 82t (Juliet Greene); 82b (Michael Paul); 84 (Christi Carter); 102 (Ron Sutherland); 104 (Bob Challinor); 107b (Juliet Greene); 112 (Michael Paul); 123 (Didier Willery). **Garden & Wildlife Matters**: 25b; 44l; 48; 78; 81b. **S & O Mathews**: 51bl; 52; 81t. **Peter McHoy**: 63tl; 69 (all). **Hugh Palmer**: 42.

The publishers would also like to thank the following for kindly allowing their gardens to be photographed:
Mr. and Mrs. D. Anderson, Suffolk; Mr. and Mrs. R. Baxter, Suffolk; Mrs. G. Calder, Suffolk; Mr. and Mrs. A. Cooper, Suffolk; Docton Mill, Devon; Mrs. B. Gillot, Suffolk; Tim Gittins, Yorkshire; Mr. and Mrs. J. Hale, Suffolk; Marwood Hill, Devon; Mill Water Gardens, Hampshire; Mrs. J. Piercy, Suffolk; Pinks Hill Landscape Merchants, Guildford; Mr and Mrs P. Robinson, Suffolk; Rosemary Rogers, Yorkshire; Rowden Nurseries, Devon; The Royal Botanic Gardens, Kew; Mr. and Mrs. P. Savage, Suffolk; Mr. and Mrs. R. Wilton, Suffolk.

The publishers would like to give special thanks to Heissner UK for lending the majority of materials and equipment featured in this book. Heissner can be contacted at The New Regency Business Centre, Common Lane Industrial Estate, Kenilworth, Warwickshire CV8 2EL (tel: 01926 851166).